# Mental Toughness Training for Soccer:
## Maximizing Technical and Mental Mechanics

**Mike Voight, Ph.D.**
**Sport Psychology-Performance Consultant**

ISBN: 978-1-58518-057-8
Library of Congress Control Number: 2007 932809
Cover design and book layout: Roger W. Rybkowski
Front cover photo: © EFE/Zuma Press
Back cover photo: Courtesy of Nick "Gator" Frilling

Coaches Choice
P.O. Box 1828
Monterey, CA 93942
www.coacheschoice.com

# Dedication

As always, to my H & S, Jenny, BC, Ally I, and Baby Julianne.

To my mentor, Dennis Viollet, who took a chance on a young coach and taught me much more than the simple game. You are greatly missed.

# Acknowledgments

I am indebted to those who have assisted me with this third book: Jim Peterson, Daniel Green, Kristi Huelsing, and the staff at Coaches Choice; my bro who is always an unbelievable source of support and inspiration; the Crew for keeping me on level ground; the coaches who gave of their time to read the book and offer important feedback; to my players at Jacksonville University and UNC Charlotte—even though we have lost touch, you will forever be remembered and talked about (for all the good times!); my Cali nephews David and Mike, who have become great athletes and great young men—I cannot wait to watch you play on TV; to my Sport Philosophy KNES 380 class at CSU-F for the inspiration for the *philosophical* athlete content; to my first soccer coaches, Johan Laurits and Tom Goodman, who were the best of role models and who inspired me to be a teacher-coach; and to Peter Haley, my soccer coach/mentor at Springfield, who taught me to expand my own capacities (especially during halftime of that Williams match!)—your lessons continue to guide me after all these years.

# Contents

# Introduction

The primary purpose of this book is to bring to light the importance of the mental aspects of playing and excelling in soccer at all competitive levels. So much has been published on improving the physical side of a soccer player's development (strength and conditioning), as well as the technical, functional, and tactical aspects. There is good reason for this, as these are the basics that every player must have as part of his game. But an often-ignored area not addressed in coaching books, videos, and seminars is the mental part of a player's game. In fact, very few resources are available that soccer coaches can turn to that specifically address mental training for their players. The following scenarios should give you a better idea of what is meant by the mental side of soccer. The number in parentheses indicates where this issue is addressed in the book.

- Players who think too much instead of just playing (Chapter 2).
- Players who are great performers at practice, yet cannot apply what they've learned come game time (Chapter 3).
- Teams or players that are consistently "slow starters" (Chapter 4).
- Players or teams that are inconsistent due to poor fitness or technical problems (Chapter 5).
- Players who are not truly committed to the team goals and standards (Chapter 6).
- Players who try to aim and force their passes or shots, thus changing their technical mechanics (Chapter 7).
- Players who do not adequately fuel or hydrate themselves (Chapter 8).
- Players who seem to "forget" set pieces (free-kicks), when they knew them all week in practice (Chapter 9).
- Teams that cannot seem to get "on the same page" (Chapter 10).
- A coach who tells a reporter that his players were just "not ready" for this game (Chapter 11).
- Players who talk and think themselves out of playing the best they can (Chapter 12).
- Players who consistently get very anxious prior to big games, and thus perform poorly due to tight muscles, negative thoughts, or poor focus (Chapter 13).
- Players who lack the inspiration to maximize their potential (Chapter 14).
- Teams that go through the motions in the majority of practices, and it shows comes game time (Chapter 15).
- Coaches who are unsure that mental training can be utilized with club players (Chapter 16).

This book goes beyond the conditioning, and beyond the X's and O's, by revealing an overlooked part of playing sound soccer—the mental game. This book introduces numerous concepts, including mental mechanics, performance barriers, expanding player capacities, mechanical breakdowns, automaticity of performing, and mental-skills training strategies. The information contained within is derived from the author's experience consulting with top performers in the sport, as well as from the most current research and applications from the sport science fields, including sport psychology, motor development, pedagogy, strength and conditioning, and exercise physiology.

This book is organized for those coaches who have specific issues in mind, as well as for those who want a broader view of all that the mental game entails. Some coaches may be dealing with team issues and want to access this information immediately, from the barriers that could be limiting team potential, to actual team intervention strategies that can be implemented right away. The book evolves from the theoretical to the practical, with Section I detailing what toughness is, followed by Section II, which explains the barriers to optimal performance, Section III, which presents proven training techniques used by top coaches, athletes, and sport psychology consultants to combat these barriers, and finally Section IV, which examines coaching effectiveness through improving training practices and coaching the mental side of the sport.

Numerous tables, figures, survey instruments, and feedback forms are included to better equip coaches with the necessary tools to combat performance barriers of all kinds. Finally, since so many inspirational sport heroes are out there representing different levels and sports, specific examples and quotes from these sources are shared throughout the book. Competitive athletes and coaches should find inspiration on a daily basis, both from within the world of sport and from outside of it.

Prior to presenting the book overview, it is important to offer some clarification. This book is written for male and female coaches, so the use of "he" is used throughout the book to simply keep the reading uniform and consistent. This style by no means indicates a sexist overtone to the writing of this text.

This book is divided into four general sections. Section I, consisting of Chapters 1 through 4, describes the many intricacies behind performance excellence—mainly talent, skill, mechanics, and automatic execution. Talent is something an individual is born with, while skill encompasses movement patterns, physical elements, and the skills of being mentally and emotional tough. Technical mechanics encapsulate the specific aspects of each task, like the many aspects of striking a ball on target. Mental and emotional toughness is defined as the ability to remain focused, energized, and confident in good times and in pressure situations. Mental mechanics, although similar to mental toughness, specifically refers to the mental processes involved with the execution of the task—mainly, the automaticity of skill execution. The important connection between the mind and the body is examined in this section as well. The final chapter in this section details the offensive and defensive mental skills, in addition to an introduction of a questionnaire that athletes can complete to determine their mental-skill strengths and weaknesses.

Section II, Chapters 5 through 7, addresses the numerous performance barriers that can interfere with a player and team fulfilling their talent and skill potential. These barriers include the physical, the technical and strategic, the numerous team barriers, and the mental and inspirational blocks. This section will conclude with a comprehensive explanation of how these barriers interfere with both technical and mental mechanical execution of passing, receiving, shooting, defending, and making and breaking plays.

Section III, Chapters 8 through 14, shows coaches and players how to successfully overcome these performance barriers so that natural talent, skills, and mechanics can dominate. Navigating players through the endless barrage of performance barriers will help to "free their minds" from "baggage" and mental interference so that they can focus instead on automatically and consistently performing the plays they have practiced over and over. Mental "skills and drills" can sometimes be thought of as being too "psychological" and therefore beyond the scope of what coaches know. This section will detail the many ways that coaches already utilize mental-skills training strategies in everyday coaching.

The last section, Section IV, includes Chapters 15 and 16. These chapters describe strategies for coaches and players to improve upon the quality of player and team practice. Since the practice setting is where the majority of the learning takes place, a direct relationship exists between the quality of practice and the quality of play on the match field. A quality of training model is detailed in this section, highlighted by a questionnaire that players can complete to gain greater insight into their practice strengths and weaknesses. The final chapter details the important elements to being the most effective coach, especially at the youth level, based upon research and presentations conducted by the author on the topic of coach effectiveness.

Just as many ways exist to teach attacking the flanks, many methods exist for improving mental toughness. Mental training goes far beyond just "thinking positive," playing "relaxed," or simply utilizing "visualization" before playing. Mastering the technical skills needed to successfully perform at the highest levels of play requires quality practice, unwavering commitment, and a drive to get better. The same holds true for wanting to be a more complete player via being a mentally tougher soccer player. Players must be committed to not only increase their awareness skills (what is working versus what is not), but also be mindful of the many performance barriers that could be interfering with their play ("why" things are not going well). The final step is to be able to respond quickly to overcome the particular barrier via specific mental-toughness techniques (the "how to" fix the performance barrier). It cannot be stated enough that continual practice of the mental-toughness training strategies detailed throughout this book is critical for any lasting effect.

The primary objective of this book is to assist players, coaches, and teams in maximizing their performance potential via a greater appreciation of the "intangibles"— namely the mental, emotional, and inspirational aspects inside every performer. Demystifying sport psychology is another objective, because so many coaches and athletes out there still do not feel that the mental aspects of their games are important, and that sport psychology principles are "hokey" or simply do not apply to them. In this book, many examples of ways that coaches actually utilize sport psychology principles in their everyday coaching practices are presented, such as pep talks, the use of video, and imagery. It is very important for coaches to see that sport psychology can be used to enhance their own coaching practices, as well as provide performance enhancement for players and teams.

The practical tips presented throughout this book are "tried and true," as they say. The author is blessed to have worked with outstanding players and coaches from the youth, collegiate, professional, and Olympic levels, who so generously shared their years of playing and coaching experiences. This book is primarily a collection of this wisdom and experience.

Applying these strategies will enable each player to perform on all cylinders, allowing natural ability, talent, and learned skills and mechanics to come through on demand, especially when it is most needed, such as in the big rivalry game, state or club championship, or national championship match!

# Section I:
# Components of Toughness

# 1

# Beyond the X's and O's: Talent, Skill, Toughness, and Mechanics

Talent, skill, toughness, and mechanics—words such as these are used in everyday conversations to evaluate the important components of player and team performance. But what do these terms really mean? They actually represent the determining factors of athletic and team-performance potential (Figure 1-1). Although talent is something that is "given" to athletes, skill, mental toughness, and mechanics are elements that can be improved upon through good coaching and diligent practice.

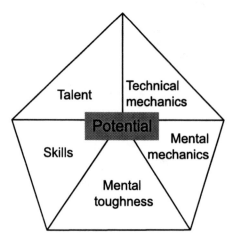

Figure 1-1. Aspects of athletic potential

The first component of athletic potential is *talent*, or a player's genetic makeup—basically what his parents have so generously given him. Whether these "gifts" are welcomed or not, they are relatively stable and beyond a player's immediate control. Talent in certain domains may not be evident at an early age (thus, the use of the term "relatively" in the previous sentence), so coaches and parents need to be careful not to jump to conclusions about future success based upon what is observed early on. The last chapter of this book details some developmental considerations for coaches who work with younger players and details appropriate expectations and talent-identification issues.

Generalized talent traits include height, weight, athleticism, speed, coordination, quickness, flexibility, agility, spatial orientation, and body type. A researcher who has studied talent identification revealed several acronyms used by professional soccer clubs that represent a list of specific criteria used to assess athletic potential (Kluka, 2004):
- TIPS: technique, intelligence, personality, and speed
- TABS: technique, attitude, balance, and speed
- SUPS: speed, understanding, personality, and skill

It is interesting to note that the evaluative criteria used by professional clubs like AJAX of the Netherlands include physical, mental, technical, and tactical attributes—all of which are believed to be important for future success. Kluka (2004) explains that a shift has taken place among researchers from talent detection—the discovery of potential performers—to talent identification, guidance, and development, thus putting the emphasis on the learning environment and quality of instruction instead of simply identifying critical attributes.

Although a particular athlete may not have been given all of the physical "gifts" of a great athlete, like the speed and agility of Michael Owens, it does not mean that he is limited in any way. All it means is that accomplishing great things on the pitch will not be as easy for him as it is for those who are "gifted" genetically. It is in such cases that qualities such as a player's work rate, drive, commitment, and toughness play an integral role.

The next component is *skill*, which players have total control over, unlike the "gift" of athletic talent. Skills are learned and can be constantly improved and enhanced. Basic movement patterns like jumping, running, backpedaling, and sprinting are all skills. Specific physical and visual motor skills include passing, controlling an air ball, dribbling with speed, seeing gaps and seams in defenses, and reacting to ever-changing situations.

Another major component of an athlete's arsenal is *technical mechanics*. Performing a task, such as switching the point of the attack, requires the synergy of numerous components that, when combined, form a motor sequence or pattern in the mind and muscles. Using the central midfielder as an example, these components, referred to as the technical mechanics of the task, include the following:

- The locomotor sequence of the task, which includes the necessary footwork and movements for the prescribed situation, such checking toward the oncoming pass to take advantage of space and time
- Postural movements, such as the proper preparation of the feet and hips for the oncoming pass
- The manipulation component, which includes receiving the ball in the direction of where it needs to go, typically away from the resistance
- Decision making, which involves the type of pass needed (ball played to feet or space), delivery speed, location, and the amount of spin
- Sensory or perceptual elements, which include the interpretation of the situation-specific cues that direct the decisions to be made, including the position of the nearest opponents. Spatial orientation is important to knowing where the opponents are positioned at all times. Vision on the pitch is a skill "worth its weight in gold."
- Conceptual elements of keeping possession or changing the attack, which include what the midfielder is focusing on prior to skill execution in terms of what he sees and how he directs his attention prior to and during the execution (too narrow a focus, too broad, or just right)

Figure 1-2. Sound technical mechanics takes the synergy of numerous processes.

Courtesy of USC Sports Information

While the prerequisite movement, physical, and visual motor skills are very important, two additional skills are needed for consistent, optimal play—*mental* and *emotional toughness.* These skills are widely recognized as being important to top performance, yet they are often ignored during practice sessions. It is often said that at the higher levels of sport, physical talent and technical skill are somewhat even among players, and it is the level of mental toughness that differentiates the best from the rest.

Jim Loehr, a mental toughness expert, has defined mental and emotional toughness as "the ability to consistently perform toward the upper range of your talent and skill regardless of competitive circumstances" (2001, pg. 5). In other words, tough players can remain confident, focused, and energized with productive emotions in pressure-filled situations, such as being down early, being fatigued, defending a quicker opponent, dealing with momentum shifts, or playing with injury.

Even in noncompetitive situations, such as during skill and drill work in practice, players should respond with intensity, focused attention, and a diligent goal-directed effort. Wanting to be mentally tough takes more than just talking about it, although doing so is a good start. Mental toughness entails being in command over inner dialogue (referred to as self-talk), thoughts, feelings, and the appraisal of situations. As you will learn, what athletes say, think, feel, and perceive can truly help or hurt their on-field performance. Mentally tough athletes think and talk tough, feel confident and energized, and perceive situations as being challenging rather than threatening. Ken Ravizza, former mental skills trainer for the Anaheim Angels and Los Angeles Dodgers, has stated that mental toughness is the ability to "be comfortable being uncomfortable." This type of athlete is able to continue playing while not allowing the mind or adversarial situation to interfere. When things get rough for this type of athlete, he is actually able to perform better because he does not allow adversity to get the best of him. Chapter 4 includes a mental toughness questionnaire, called the Offensive and Defensive Mental Skills Survey, that alerts players to the specific mental-emotional toughness skills that they may be lacking.

Although mental toughness is usually applied to the individual player, teams can work toward a collective toughness. Chapter 10 addresses ways to improve team unity and cohesion, as well as help teams accept a common vision and identity.

The final component to athletic potential is *mental mechanics.* Each player on the field performs different skill tasks depending upon his position and his specific assignment on each play. The specific motor programs needed to execute these different tasks are developed over time at practice through quality, repetitive training. For players to take what they do repeatedly in practice onto the game field, each mechanical component must be taught, practiced, evaluated, and practiced over and over again. Once players begin to master the nuances of each technical skill, game situations and game simulations should then be introduced. Incorporating technical mechanics into everyday teaching will better prepare players for quality execution in practice and at game time. The next step is for players to be able to execute these motor programs automatically, without having to think about what to do and how to do it. This automatic processing, or mental mechanics, is a major determinant of optimal, consistent play, which is why automatic execution should be the goal of any performer.

Each player's faith in his own talent, skills, mental toughness, and quality training is at the core of automatic performances, and thus is the central theme of this book. Chapter 2 goes into greater detail about how technical and mental mechanics are linked and how to sharpen them to improve execution and automaticity of action.

Courtesy of USC Sports Information

Figure 1-3. Playing automatically entails letting go of conscious control and just going for it!

# Chapter Summary

- Athletic potential consists of numerous determining variables, including talent, skill components, and technical and mental mechanics.
- Two very important skills that can and should be improved and practiced are mental and emotional toughness.
- Mental and emotional toughness are defined as the ability to be resilient, confident, focused, and energized in times of pressure and adversity.
- Coaching the technical mechanics of a skill involves more than just the physical components (e.g., footwork, preparation movements, and manipulation). Being able to base decisions on the interpretation of situation-specific cues and then executing the skills based upon this information are critical ingredients to effective execution. Mental mechanics is the ability of athletes to execute the technical mechanics of a task without overthinking or allowing distractions to interfere.

# 2

# Technical and Mental Mechanics: Automatic Processing

When players are first learning how to pass, kick, dribble, and control the ball, they must concentrate on all the little details, beginning with the demonstration of the desired skill, the critical instruction phrases from the coach or trainer, and the continual practice reps. After each correction, this process is repeated over and over. In the beginning, they can only do one skill aspect at a time. As they progress, a lot of conscious thinking is still being conducted, yet common mistakes dwindle. Once players begin to master the particular technical mechanics of the skill, they begin to perform the skill sequence without having to think about each little piece, which is referred to as mental mechanics. Instead, a motor program has been developed and muscle memory leads the way. This ability to "free the mind" and not think through the skill during execution is a valuable aspect to consistent, optimal play.

An analogy that is often used to describe this process is teaching a teenager how to drive a car. The first time behind the wheel is scary for all parties involved. The driver is narrowly focused, or has "tunnel vision," because he is trying to remember each step of the process, beginning with putting on the seat belt, turning the ignition, putting it into reverse, and looking in all directions before backing out. Once he gets out of the driveway, the real adventure begins. External stimuli, which include other cars, pedestrians, crossings, lights, and signs, are in need of immediate and constant attention, not to mention the continual checks of car speed and looks in the mirrors. Internal distractions are also present, including fears and anxieties about driving a car

Figure 2-1. Learning skills for the first time entails conscious thought and lots of practice.

for the first time. But after numerous trials, the countless steps and potential distractions seem to disappear, as the new driver is suddenly able to keep the car on the road while selecting the next tune on the CD player or having a conversation with passengers without really thinking. This example illustrates how automatic processing occurs due to the synergy between physical, technical, and mental processes that result through continual, quality practice.

In both of these examples, the performer, whether it a beginning player or a beginning driver, had to think through each of their specific actions to get the job done. Yet once they began to learn the necessary skills, the body and mind takes over all of the execution processes, signifying efficient technical mechanics, and no longer requires continual focus, indicating sound mental mechanics.

Keep in mind that even top-level athletes go through this learning process whenever a change is made to their technical mechanics. In some situations, especially when an athlete is struggling through a performance slump, changes are made to an already established mechanical program. As a side note, this technique is usually not the method recommended to reverse the deleterious effects of a performance slump. In most cases, making changes will only lead to more mechanical problems, since these changes are usually not practiced as extensively as needed. For example, when an otherwise consistent skill, such as dribbling, bending crossed balls, or passing, all of a sudden becomes inconsistent, it could be caused by a physical, mental, or emotional barrier, rather than a technical problem. Section II details numerous performance barriers that could initially cause, or assist in continuing, performance slumps.

To fully integrate even the most minute change, the athlete must focus intently on each piece of the process, much like he had to do when just starting out. Yet when these slight adjustments are made, mistakes will become an important part of the process and should not be fretted over in the short term. Changes to skill execution must be made only when sufficient practice time exists to incorporate these alterations. With continual quality practice, changes are integrated and the desired performance results occur. Tiger Woods, arguably the best golfer in the world, has made significant changes to his swing throughout the years, even after winning his first Masters. With each change came hours and hours of focused practice attempting to revise an already established and successfully consistent motor program. The great ones, like Roger Clemens, Tracy McGrady, Brett Favre, David Beckham, Michael Owen, and Ronaldinho, are always looking to achieve another level of greatness. Making such changes is risky for most athletes, because of the time needed to institute change. Even the great ones must devote practice time to integrating the new elements before automatic processing can be assured.

*"You can't miss nor can you wait to get to the next green. Pretty soon you're on autopilot, playing by instinct and feel. That's as close to finding your own game as you can get. Sometimes we think too much instead of trusting that inner voice that says you can do it."*
—Tiger Woods, Four-time Master's Winner
(2001, p. 259)

Automatic processing, or what Tiger terms "autopilot," can be quite unstable due to the many factors that act to sabotage the process. Section II details the voluminous barriers that interfere with automatic execution. The strength of an athlete's mental toughness and mental mechanics is tested when confronted with these performance barriers. Performers who are able to successfully defend themselves against the damaging effects of performance barriers will be much more consistent in pressure-packed game situations than those who are "beginners" in terms of their mental toughness and mental mechanics.

For example, one of these performance barriers is attentional capacity. How much an athlete can focus on at one time is actually quite limited, especially in the presence of hundreds of potential visual and auditory distractions. Yet among the stimuli bombarding the player, some are needed to effectively execute the next play. Goalkeepers look for key cues around the ball, as well cues on the strong- and weaksides, to decide their optional position. The same can be said about other positional players who utilize cues from the environment to get their respective jobs done. Proficiency at focusing in this manner entails not only knowing what cues to attend to, but also being able to let go of "clutter" that may interfere with this processing. An entire array of performance barriers is addressed in Section II.

How does a player work to improve upon technical and mental mechanics so that "clutter" of this kind does not interfere with performance? The answer lies in knowing how to maximize the mind-body connection, which is at the core of the sport psychology principles presented throughout this book. Maximizing the connection between the *mind*—which encompasses thoughts, self-talk, attitudes, feelings, motives, and perceptions—and the *body*—which consists of physical sensations, emotional reactions, technical proficiency, and physical performances—entails conscious awareness of how this connection works. Chapter 3 provides the information necessary to enhance awareness of how the mind can help, yet also hurt, athletic performance. An applied model is then presented to describe what coaches and players can do to utilize this mind-body connection to their advantage and maximize performance.

Courtesy of UMASS Sports Information

Figure 2-2. Coaches and players are both responsible for maximizing the mind-body connection to enhance play.

# Chapter Summary

- Automatic processing results when athletes can let go of conscious thoughts and allow their skills, talent, and practice to take over.
- Whenever experienced players make even the most subtle changes to an established technical skill, they should expect some delay in playing to their former level because of the relearning process. Performance in practice will include some miscues until the new skill component becomes automatic, which takes continual quality practice and game-simulated practice.
- Performance barriers can sabotage a player's automatic execution of even the most well-learned skills.
- Being more aware of how the mind and body work to help and hurt athletic performances is a critical lesson to learn if optimal, consistent performance is a goal.

# 3

# The Mind-Body Connection: Maximizing the Capacity for Excellence

*"Nowhere is it more abundantly clear than in competitive sports that everything is interconnected. What you think, how you act, what you eat, how much you sleep, your fighting spirit, your fitness, your passion for life are all intimately connected."*

—Jim Loehr, Ed.D., Former Coach and Mental Skills Trainer (2001)

*"If you as a coach are good at analyzing and adjusting the mental and emotional state of your team, then you will win many matches against coaches who don't understand it."*

—Pete Waite, Volleyball Coach, Wisconsin (Waite, 2002, p. 306)

*"You get out what you put in … you can't be half in and half out. Coaches don't say the game is 90 percent mental for the hell of it."*

—Mike Stoops, Head Football Coach, Arizona (Dufresne, 2004, p. D12)

These quotes typify what some coaches believe about the application of mental-skills training to their chosen sport. How common is it to hear or read in interviews with coaches and players about mental issues contributing to wins or losses? Sound bites such as, "We just weren't in it tonight," or "We didn't do the little things," or even "We started out too flat and couldn't climb out of the hole we dug because of it" are quite common. Conversely, coaches also cite mental or team factors after wins, including "We played as a team tonight," "We stayed positive despite some early troubles," or "We stayed focused on the game plan and executed."

Despite the growth of the sport-psychology field in the past decade, and the increase in the number of teams and athletes who utilize sport-psychology consultants, some misconceptions still exist regarding the mental aspects of sport. Chapter 11 describes the many ways that coaches and players already apply sport psychology principles to the game. Teaching and practicing the mental side of soccer can be integrated into everyday coaching practices, especially if coaches realize that they are already doing so.

The following questions bring up specific situations that provide more evidence of how the mind-body link affects soccer performance.

- Does it appear that sometimes players "forget" how to execute well-learned skills and plays?
- How often do players fall short of fulfilling their performance potential?
- How often do players talk negatively about themselves before, during, or after play?
- Do the team members consider themselves to be part of a slow-starting team? How about a come-from-behind team?
- Do players play well after making mistakes?
- Do players play poorly on the road?
- Do they play well under pressure?
- How many players are good practice players but fall short when it comes to game time?
- Does it appear that sometimes players quit trying after experiencing adversity?
- Do players know what specific areas of their games are strengths and which areas are in need of improvement?

These questions bring to the forefront the important connections between the mind and the body. They also refer to 10 specific mind-body connections. How many of the following scenarios play themselves out during the course of a season with your team or players?

- *Does it appear that sometimes players "forget" how to execute well-learned skills and plays?* An excess of anxiety can affect concentration, memory, and the execution of well-learned skills and tactics. Anxiety can also create physical tension or increase mental interference, and in turn affect confidence levels and ultimately performance.

Figure 3-1. The mental aspects of soccer are acknowledged yet seldom practiced.

- *How often do players fall short of fulfilling their performance potential? In what specific areas do players and teams fall short?* The topic of expanding upon player capacities for performance excellence is detailed later in this chapter.
- *How often do players talk negatively about themselves before, during, or after play?* Negative self-talk affects confidence, motivation, competitive focus, anxiety, and performance, both directly and indirectly.
- *Do the team members consider themselves to be part of a slow-starting team? How about a come-from-behind team?* The use of one-trial generalizations, or the labeling of strengths or weaknesses based upon one outcome, is a troublesome practice. For example, if a team begins a game by giving up an early goal but then wins in the end, the players may declare to others that they are "slow starters." This declaration can set into motion a "self-fulfilling prophecy" whereby this team always starts out slowly, leaving to chance the ability to pull out the victory on a consistent basis. Using the self-fulfilling prophecy in a productive way is definitely recommended, such as the belief that the team is a fast-starting one, or that the team is able to finish off opponents.
- *Do players play well after making mistakes?* Most players who are not able to let go of mistakes will continue making the same mistakes. It is like playing with a "monkey on your back," with the burden weighing a player down and making it more difficult to play automatically. Players who have not prepared for potential setbacks, via refocusing or coping routines, will continue to allow mistakes to knock them off of their games.

- *Do players play poorly on the road?* Finding ways to focus on the job at hand will often lead to a "silencing of the crowd" through solid play and execution, thereby drawing players' attention away from a hostile environment.
- *Do they play well under pressure?* Helping players realize what they do and do not have control over can help them focus on what needs to be done presently, regardless of the situation and their anxiety level.
- *How many players are good practice players but fall short when it comes to game time?* Great practice players can sometimes lose something when it comes to game time. Fears and anxieties take center stage, mixed with an inability to cope with performance barriers. Talent, skill, and mental mechanics will forever be hindered if these barriers are not overcome.
- *Does it appear that sometimes players quit trying after experiencing adversity?* Adversity, whether it comes in the form of being down big early or late, losing a key starter to injury, or bad officiating calls must be overcome. Having organized plans to deal with potential adversity is one method. Another is to be in better control of emotional reactions to adversity.
- *Do players know what specific areas of their games are strengths and which areas are in need of improvement?* Players who are not aware of what works for them and what does not tend to "go through the motions" in practice, since they do not have adequate direction regarding the route to consistent, optimal performance.

These questions accentuate the importance of how players think and talk to themselves prior to, during, and after performing, as well as the impact these thoughts and self-dialogue have on actions, physical sensations (tension, relaxation), behaviors, feelings, and ultimately performance. Additionally, how players emotionally react to pressure situations and adversity can either adversely affect or improve upon their performance.

> "Sometimes you can find yourself falling off track and going to the negative side of things... You just have to keep a positive attitude about everything."
>
> —Fred Taylor, Running Back, Jacksonville Jaguars (NFL)
> (Stellino, 2002, p. D10)

Although the previous questions are used primarily to assess weaknesses that some players or teams may have with the interconnection between the mind and body, these same questions can also highlight strengths. Players who transfer the work done on the training ground to the match field usually do not get rattled under pressure or adversity and continue to work hard under duress. This success is the result of solid mental and emotional toughness and sound mental mechanics. As discussed in Chapter 1, some players inherit the talent necessary for optimal play, including physical, technical, and mental skills, while others have to work extremely hard to maximize the gifts they have been given.

Very few players, however, especially at the middle school, high school, and college levels, truly have *complete* games. For this reason, most teams (or players) employ coaches of all types to help players improve upon all areas of their game and progress toward becoming complete players. These coaches can range from positional, strength, speed, and flexibility coaches to nutrition experts and even dance teachers who help players improve agility and footwork. Occasionally, a sport psychologist is hired to speak to the team, albeit only one or two times during a season. Although the use of specialists can be quite beneficial, coaches can help each one of their athletes become complete players by coaching not just the physical and technical aspects of soccer, but the mental game as well.

An applied model that can be employed by coaches at all competitive levels to help expand upon their players' overall games, or capacities, is shown in Figure 3-2. As indicated, the pyramid-shaped model represents the seven categories critical to

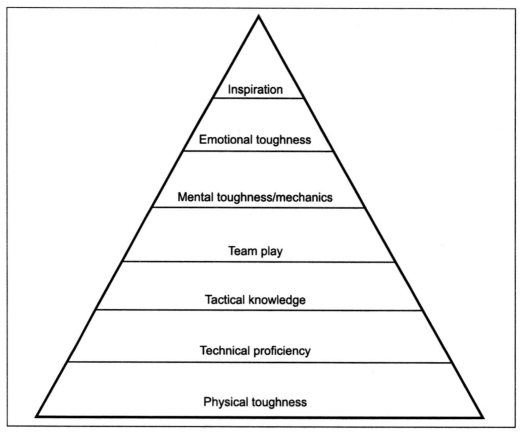

Figure 3-2. Expand player capacities for more complete individual games.

optimal performance. The lower sections of the pyramid represent those areas that are trained on a regular basis, are deemed most important by coaches, and are easier to "fix." The areas toward the top of the pyramid represent those aspects that are trained less frequently and are more difficult to master, especially without adequate information and strategies. Coaches have put a heavy emphasis on helping athletes maximize their physical, technical, and tactical abilities. Hopefully, this book encourages coaches to put a greater emphasis on the other aspects of coaching/playing sound soccer.

Although some coaches do emphasize the importance of team unity and effectiveness, an important challenge for coaches is to assist players in expanding their *mental, emotional,* and *inspirational* capacities. Maximizing performance capacities will enable players to play closer to their full potential, by sharpening their skills and mechanical strengths while also improving upon their weaker areas. Before this improvement can be made, players must be aware of their strengths and weaknesses.

*"The pursuit of excellence begins with getting to know your own patterns. This is simply a process of becoming more aware of your own capacities, strengths, and weaknesses. It also means becoming more aware of what you really want, as opposed to what others want of you."*
—Terry Orlick, Ph.D., Mental Skills Trainer, Author
(2000, p. 79)

Performance capacities are defined by a list of qualities that can be seen by coaches and players alike. Players and teams who show these particular qualities are close to maximizing their capacity in the specified area. For example, a player who is as strong and fit as they can be is maximizing his physical capacity, and thus, improves his chances for success. Players who are "complete" players can honestly report that they fulfill their capacities across these seven performance areas. However, those players who do not employ these practices are falling shy of fulfilling their capacities, and lowering their chances at succeeding daily in practice and weekly on the game field.

# Physical Capacity

Signs of maximizing physical capacity include the following:
- Players who maximally prepare their "machines" for practice and games by eating what they should and ensuring proper hydration.
- Players who physically prepare in the off-season across all fitness components: strength, endurance, speed, flexibility, aerobic endurance, power, agility, body composition, and vertical jump.

- Players who provide themselves with adequate rest and recovery, and stretch between practices and games.
- Players who do not allow fatigue to inhibit their play.

*"20–30% of the game is spent moving at a fairly high speed, with frequent changes in direction…with players covering 6.2 miles in a full 90-minute match… Training should be specific to meet these needs."*
                                                        —Dr. Don Kirkendall (1996, p. 50)

Fitness is a part of a player's performance that is totally within his control. Players can be as fit as they want to be; they just need to put in the necessary time and effort. Chapter 5 details the many physical barriers that could limit players from expanding their physical toughness capacities, and Chapter 8 describes how players and coaches can effectively combat these barriers.

# Technical Capacity

Behavioral indicators of maximizing technical capacity include the following:
- Players who know what specific technical skills they are in need of improving and actively train those areas at game speed.
- Players who practice on their own, and ask for help from coaches, to improve particular technical aspects.
- Players who focus on the mechanical aspects of the skill when learning something new, or when adding a new "wrinkle" to a previously learned skill.
- Players who are consistent with their positional skills.

Chapter 1 lists the many technical mechanics involved in a skill, including the locomotor sequencing, manipulation components, and the perceptual and conceptual elements that should be included in everyday teaching and subsequent repetition training. Players who are able to pinpoint, on their own, the specific mechanical areas that went awry after mistakes or poor execution, will be better able to make necessary corrections on the court during the flow of play and practice. Empowering athletes with this type of awareness, called self-regulation in the sport-psychology literature, can be invaluable to a player's development.

# Tactical Capacity

Behavioral indicators of maximizing tactical capacity include the following:
- Players who know all the necessary plays and reads that make up their specific *offensive* assignments (e.g., overlapping runs, combination passing and

movement, playing to target player's feet) and *defensive* assignments (e.g., goalside coverage, drop toward the ballside when defending weakside opponents, delay when defending numbers-down).

- Players who internalize what they see from game tape and the scouting reports regarding their positions and roles and then implement what they learn during training and match play.
- Players who also know some of what their teammates are doing, or should be doing, in certain cases.

Jacob Rogers, a former tackle on the two-time national champion USC football team, was quoted in a *Los Angeles Times* article as saying, "My dad always taught me to learn what everyone around you is supposed to do, because when you get into game time, situations happen and you might have to help somebody out" (September 24, 2003a). True students of the game adopt these tactical qualities and attempt to maximize their tactical knowledge and applications.

# Team Capacity

Behavioral indicators of maximizing team capacity include the following:
- Players who are willing to sacrifice individual acclaim for team pursuits.
- Players who hold themselves accountable for their behaviors and actions.
- Teams that are committed to the same goals and accept what it will take to get there.
- Team members who know and accept their roles.
- Players who help to motivate and inspire their teammates to get better.
- Players who are able to communicate with their coaches and teammates.
- Teams who "buy into" the coaches' system and help each other adhere to the accompanying standards.

Most coaches know what the "disease of me" is and how it can ruin a team's pursuit of excellence. Pat Riley, former Lakers "Showtime" coach and current Miami Heat coach, originally coined this phrase in his 1993 book. Are your players willing to sacrifice the "me" for the "we"? Do you have players who are more about their individual numbers and accomplishments than the collective efforts of the team? Without an honest commitment to the team ethic, teams will fail to play up to their expectations and potential.

Players need to make a conscious effort to be not only "coachable," but also good team players. "Putting the team first" is a common phrase that coaches use to impress this need upon their players, but how many players actually practice this philosophy on a daily basis? Being a team player is a skill that must be practiced, just like any technical

Courtesy of USC Sports Information

Figure 3-3. Maximizing individual and team capacities takes a lot of hard work, but the rewards will be well worth it.

or mental skill. Chapter 10 discusses team-building practices, which consist of activities for players and coaches to improve their ability to put the team pursuit before their personal agendas.

# Mental Capacity

Behavioral indicators of maximizing mental capacity—or building character in action—include the following:

- Players who look to the mental side of their games to gain an edge over their opponents by setting goals; imagining success; using intensity-control techniques, concentration, and focus for the full 90 minutes; having quality practice sessions; putting the team first; and communicating with coaches and teammates.

> *"Mental toughness is many things and rather difficult to explain. Its qualities are sacrifice and self-denial. Also, most importantly, it is combined with a perfectly disciplined will that refuses to give in. It's a state of mind—you could call it character in action."*
> —Vince Lombardi, Hall of Fame Football Coach (Dorfman, 2003, p. 165)

- Players who are consistently able to remain confident, regardless of how they, or their team, are performing.
- Players who are consistently able to prepare and ready themselves to play against any opponent, and thus, are not as likely to play "down" to the level of competition.
- Players who remain focused on their specific roles for the upcoming sequence, rather than being distracted by past mistakes or worries about what the next touch will bring.
- Players who are successfully able to not only let go of mistakes, but also learn from them and ready themselves for the next possession.
- Players who are able to motivate themselves to play their "A" games, regardless of the opponent, and be able to consistently give their best efforts throughout practice sessions.
- Players who are able to consistently prepare and ready themselves to practice and play to their maximum, which includes dealing with their confidence, anxiety, fears, worries, tension, and negative moods.
- Players who are consistently able to "let go" of conscious control over their mechanics and allow themselves to trust their skills and simply "go for it," rather than thinking their way through execution.

Mental toughness is defined as the ability to remain confident, focused, energized, and composed in all types of performance situations, especially pressure situations. Being able to rise to the occasion in big games is tantamount to being a top competitor, but so is raising the level of motivation, effort, and execution during a tedious drill, doing basic reps of a needed skill, or finding energy during the second hour of practice. Players who are able to rise to all of these occasions are truly mentally tough competitors—and are players coaches love to coach.

Athletes who are mentally tough are easy to spot, since they are the ones who get the ball when big plays need to be made. These players lead the team via their words and actions. Most players at the higher levels of the game are so into themselves and their own games that it shows something special when players are able to take care of themselves, yet also offer to help their teammates excel to the utmost of their capabilities. These players also perform consistently well, regardless of what is going on around them. A consistent competitor who knows a thing or two about mental toughness is Tiger Woods. In his book, *How I Play Golf,* he detailed his five "building blocks to mental toughness" (pp. 258–259):

- Learn from the positive and negatives from your performances.
- Take ownership of your mistakes. You are the one who is responsible for them.
- Never repeat mistakes.
- Be able to turn negatives into positives.
- After tough outings, don't beat yourself up too much, because plenty of people will do it for you.

No real secrets are offered in this list. The difference between Tiger and the rest of the field is that he actually does these things instead of simply reading them.

## Emotional Capacity

Behavioral indicators of maximizing emotional capacity include the following:

- Players who are consistently able to deal well with unexpected events, such as lineup changes due to injuries or performance slumps, broken plays, a change in formations, and routine alterations, such as inclement weather or arriving late to the game due to transportation problems.
- Players who are able to cope with frustration over making mistakes, poor play, and other adversities, such as coaches' decisions, teammates' actions, or officials' calls.
- Players who are able to remain strong and resilient when fatigued or nursing minor aches and pains.
- Players who are able to free their minds (e.g., fears and anxieties), and control their emotions so that they can play with all of their talents and skills.
- Players and teams who have the ability to consistently deal with momentum changes. Soccer is a game predicated on momentum swings. Teams that are able to sustain momentum when they have it, and regain it when it is lost, have the best chance of succeeding.

Operating to the fullest emotional capacity entails the ability to take risks and not fear the potential negative consequences of these risks. According to Saul Miller (2003), sport psychology consultant for several NHL teams, fear has many faces: "fear of failure, fear of embarrassment, fear of not meeting expectations, fear of letting the team down, fear of getting hurt, fear of losing control, fear of the unknown, and even fear of success" (p. 81). Players who lack emotional toughness are fearful of so many things, especially of being discovered as not very good players. This lack of internal confidence is quite common, even among those players who "talk" great games and are very boastful of their playing. Talking themselves up in this fashion helps keep the "critics" at bay, while protecting their deflated confidence and keeping these insecurities beneath the surface. Methods players can use to improve their internal confidence are addressed throughout this book, but especially in Chapter 12.

Players who are emotionally tough play all-out and never worry about what others are thinking or saying about them or their play. These players do not "handicap" themselves by coming up with excuses prior to playing, such as: "I'm not feeling my best today," "My ankle is still a little tender," "I'm still getting over that cold," or "I don't play well in this park." If a less emotionally tough player fails to dominate, and their critics begin thinking that the player is not a *player*, these excuses can be used as a shield to deflect the criticism and protect his image as a top-notch player.

# Inspirational Capacity

Behavioral indicators of maximizing inspirational capacity include the following:
- Players who truly *love* playing soccer and their specific positions.
- Players who are consistently "into it" and do all that is necessary to improve upon their individual play.
- Players who willingly make sacrifices of their time, their bodies, and their social activities for the sake of their individual pursuit.
- Players who know exactly why they play soccer and what they plan to accomplish in the sport.
- Players who find inspiration from a multitude of sources, including their own maximal efforts, teammates, coaches, and other outside sources that could include other players, past coaches and teammates, and news articles.
- Players who have an appreciation for their playing philosophy and "practice what they preach." They are ethical, process-focused, and able to balance their sport with other important aspects of their lives, including school, family, jobs, and friends. They also know that they are more than just soccer players.

*"Personal excellence is largely a question of believing in your own capacities and fully committing yourself to your own development."*
—Terry Orlick, Ph.D., Mental Skill Trainer/Author (2000, p. 40)

In a *Los Angeles Times* article, Eric Crouch, former Nebraska quarterback and 2001 Heisman Trophy winner, announced his decision to quit pro football after stints with St. Louis and Green Bay (July, 2003b). He stated that, "I just couldn't get excited about it. I couldn't be passionate about it." It seemed as though Eric Crouch lost his inspiration to play. How many players on your team appear to have lost their inspiration to play and improve? Players who simply go through the motions in practice are those who lose sight of their goals and aspirations, and are not willing to commit their talents, abilities, and efforts. Much more is discussed regarding what drives and inspires players in Chapter 6.

Figure 3-4. Having a more complete game can help players achieve great things.

The sections of the pyramid in Figure 3-2 are expanded upon in Figure 3-7, in which each section contains questions for players to answer that can help them gain a better awareness of their present capacity level. Before a player can operate to his maximal capacities, he must be aware of his current level and how far it may be from his top effort. If the majority of your players' responses to the questions are "no," it indicates that they are not working toward maximizing their specific capacities. Responses marked with a "yes" indicate progress toward becoming a complete player who plays a complete game.

Upon getting responses from each player and/or the team as a whole, individual/team meetings with players can be conducted to discuss specific areas that players need to commit to improving, as well as to list the players' areas of strengths. Coaches who take the time to talk about specific ways to maximize each athlete's capacities show the athletes how committed they are in assisting the players in their pursuit. The critical piece to this model is that your athletes and the team are being asked the "right" questions—questions that range across the seven different capacities.

**Inspiration**
- What do you love about the game?
- What are your reasons for playing the game and position?
- What makes you the happiest while playing?
- What is your playing philosophy?
- What drives you? What do you want to accomplish?

**Emotional toughness**
- Are you a risk taker?
- Do you deal well with changes?
- Do you try new ways to improve your game?
- Do you cope well with your frustration?

**Mental toughness/mechanics**
- Do you use a pre-practice or pre-game routine?
- Does your focus fade during practice or games?
- Are you confident regardless of how you're playing?
- Do you stay positive (self talk, thoughts) when you're not playing well?

**Team play**
- Are you honestly committed to the team goals?
- Do you and your positional teammates think as one?
- Do you make positive contributions to the team every day?
- Do you feel connected to teammates and coaches?

**Tactical knowledge**
- Do you know the demands of your position?
- Do you know all of your positional responsibilities?
- Do you know the positional responsibilities of teammates?
- Do you look for your opponent's weaknesses/tendencies?

**Technical proficiency**
- Do you know your technical strengths and weaknesses?
- Do you practice on your own to improve?
- Do you know the specific technical elements that are faulty?
- Are the majority of your practices quality sessions?

**Physical toughness**
- Do you adequately fuel and hydrate your "machine" each day?
- Do you ensure that you get proper sleep before games and practices?
- Do you work to improve upon your flexibility?
- Do you put in maximal effort on your conditioning training?

Figure 3-5. Capacity for excellence questions

Another exercise is to ask your players to determine the percentage of their mistakes that are due to each of these seven components. For example, if a player makes the majority of his mistakes because he is always a step too late or too slow, he may need to improve upon his first-step speed and agility (physical capacity). Those players who struggle with committing too many errors due to their frustration need to work on coping more effectively with their emotions (emotional capacity).

Figure 3-6. Being frustrated and making mistakes is just another part of the game. Players who can move forward sidestep several barriers that could have a deleterious effect on their games.

Another activity is to have players brainstorm why they have not been able to accomplish their preferred goals due to barriers in these seven components. Then the players should be asked to brainstorm some solutions to these barriers. The feedback gathered during these exercises can be an important foundation for subsequent team goal-setting sessions targeting solutions to common team problems and barriers.

Once players know what needs improving, beginning with those areas that are easier to strengthen (physical, technical, and tactical), coaches and available support staff can then offer their expertise in providing athletes with the means to bring about change via specific strategies and tools. Assistant coaches, strength coaches, trainers, and nutritionists can be valuable in improving physical toughness (strength and conditioning, recovery, and energization), whereas a sport-psychology consultant can help strengthen team, mental, emotional, and inspirational toughness.

Since the coaching staff knows the players best, their input and suggestions will be paramount, as well as their continual follow-up and feedback to the athlete and the team as a whole. Although the use of sport-psychology consultants can be very valuable (more valuable if you utilize an experienced, knowledgeable, professionally trained and educated certified consultant with sound sport experience), some teams do not have the access or means to utilize these services. Coaches have utilized, and will continue to incorporate, sport-psychology practices into their everyday coaching. Reading this book indicates a desire to improve upon your knowledge of sport psychology–coach effectiveness. Chapter 11 details the many ways coaches incorporate mental-skills training into their everyday coaching.

Section II delves deeper into the seven performance areas by specifying the numerous barriers that players face when trying to perform to the utmost of their physical, technical, tactical, team, mental, emotional, and inspirational capacities. Section III discusses tested methods used to combat these barriers to consistent, optimal performance.

# Chapter Summary

- How players think and talk to themselves prior to, during, and after games can be a great advantage or disadvantage, depending upon the content of these cognitions (thoughts) and self-talk. For most players, positive and productive thoughts and self-talk help performance, while negative thoughts and self-talk hinder top performance.
- For players to have "complete" games, coaches must teach not only the physical and technical aspects of soccer, but also the mental and emotional game.
- Players who are "complete" players maximize their capacities across seven performance areas—physical, technical, tactical, team, mental, emotional, and inspirational.
- Before players can maximize their performance capacities, they must be aware of their current level and how far it is from their top effort.
- Although support staff can be valuable in helping players maximize their capacities to have more complete games, coaches are the critical pieces to the puzzle. Even the slightest knowledge of sport-psychology principles and techniques will be of great assistance if it is passed along to players.

# 4

# Offensive and Defensive Mental Toughness Skills

This book is meant to help coaches maximize players' performances by maximizing their capacities, which range from the physical to the inspirational. Chapter defines these capacities, and subsequent chapters will outline performance barriers that exist within each capacity along with strategies that can be used to combat these barriers. This chapter delves deeper into evaluating strengths and weaknesses within the mental and emotional capacities, since these two areas are recognized as being important for consistent performance.

Sean McCann, director of sport psychology services at the United States Olympic Training Center, presented a model of mental skills that "explains why athletes need mental skills and how they work in various sport situations…. The model aids in making invisible mental skills become more visible" (2002, p. 11). This model is effective in presenting the importance of mental-skills training as well as the application of training strategies to your players and fellow coaches.

The numerous mental skills are divided into two main categories: offensive mental skills and defensive mental skills. Since soccer players appreciate the importance of the defensive and offensive sides of the game, this model speaks with the jargon that players are used to hearing on a daily basis. Just as soccer teams need to be solid on both sides of the ball to be successful, athletes who are driven to succeed must have sharp offensive and defensive mental skills. McCann (2002) defines *offensive* skills as those that allow players to perform to the top of their capacities, and thereby dominate their performances. These skills include confidence, competitive focus, preparation, planning, readiness, visualization, and quality training. *Defensive* skills enable players to remain composed and resilient in the face of adversity. Skills such as the ability to refocus and recover from adversity, control emotions and energy levels, and "look" ready for the next play make up the defensive mental skills.

# Offensive and Defensive Mental Skills Survey

Players may be strong in some of the mental skills, yet weak in others. The first step is to identify these areas of strength and weakness. The Offensive and Defensive Mental Skills Survey is a valuable tool to acquire this information (Voight, 2004) (Figure 4-1). This questionnaire is divided into numerous sections, each representing a key mental skill. These skills are defined by their influence on performance.

## Offensive Mental Skills

- Confidence—the ability to trust the abilities and skills, and perform automatically, without thought or hesitation
- Competitive focus—the ability to remain focused on important performance cues that are necessary for successful execution
- Mental preparation—the ability to think in the present and not worry about past mistakes or future performances; thoughts and self-talk are focused on the process of improving, not on outcome or results
- Quality of training—training that is process-focused, goal-directed, and performed with maximal effort
- Use of imagery—the ability to see playing excellence, which can aid in confidence enhancement, preparation, and emotional control prior to and during play

## Defensive Mental Skills

- Refocus—the ability to get back on track by focusing on game-related cues rather than on internal or external distractions
- Recovery—the ability to expeditiously deal with setbacks and get back to a "ready," optimal state via thoughts and feelings
- Intensity control—the ability to control debilitating tension, thoughts, and self-talk to help stay on task and remain process-focused
- Physical presentation—the ability to look stoic and confident, regardless of the situation, such as being down early, experiencing a slump, missing tackles, or striking erroneous crossed balls

## Offensive and Defensive Mental Skills Survey

Please complete each sentence, and then respond by circling the number that corresponds with the most appropriate word.

**KEY:**

Never: 0     Very rarely: 1     Rarely: 2     Sometimes: 3     Often: 4     Very often: 5     Always: 6

|  |  | never |  |  |  |  | always |  |
|---|---|---|---|---|---|---|---|---|
| 1. | I _____ worry about making mistakes. | 0 | 1 | 2 | 3 | 4 | 5 | 6 |
| 2. | I _____ have a very difficult time letting go of mistakes. | 0 | 1 | 2 | 3 | 4 | 5 | 6 |
| 3. | I _____ bounce back quickly from setbacks. | 0 | 1 | 2 | 3 | 4 | 5 | 6 |
| 4. | I _____ dwell on mistakes and "carry them" with me to the next play. | 0 | 1 | 2 | 3 | 4 | 5 | 6 |
| 5. | I _____ consider myself a confident player. | 0 | 1 | 2 | 3 | 4 | 5 | 6 |
| 6. | When I'm not playing well, I _____ get negative and get down on myself. | 0 | 1 | 2 | 3 | 4 | 5 | 6 |
| 7. | On the field I _____ project a confident image regardless of the score. | 0 | 1 | 2 | 3 | 4 | 5 | 6 |
| 8. | At critical times in games I _____ find myself thinking negatively. | 0 | 1 | 2 | 3 | 4 | 5 | 6 |
| 9. | I _____ find myself getting too nervous/anxious before/during games. | 0 | 1 | 2 | 3 | 4 | 5 | 6 |
| 10. | I _____ do my best when the pressure is on. | 0 | 1 | 2 | 3 | 4 | 5 | 6 |
| 11. | I _____ find it difficult to get energized to play a lesser team. | 0 | 1 | 2 | 3 | 4 | 5 | 6 |
| 12. | I _____ have poor focus when I have to make a critical play. | 0 | 1 | 2 | 3 | 4 | 5 | 6 |
| 13. | I _____ get distracted during a match. | 0 | 1 | 2 | 3 | 4 | 5 | 6 |
| 14. | I _____ think too much while I play, instead of just playing. | 0 | 1 | 2 | 3 | 4 | 5 | 6 |
| 15. | Poor officiating (calls), rowdy spectators, or opponent's behaviors _____ takes me off my game. | 0 | 1 | 2 | 3 | 4 | 5 | 6 |
| 16. | I _____ get anxious (hope I don't choke) the crazier it gets in competition (weather, score, opponent behavior). | 0 | 1 | 2 | 3 | 4 | 5 | 6 |
| 17. | I am _____ a "slow starter," meaning that it takes me a while to get "into the rhythm" of the game. | 0 | 1 | 2 | 3 | 4 | 5 | 6 |
| 18. | I _____ use a set pre-practice or pre-game routine to improve readiness. | 0 | 1 | 2 | 3 | 4 | 5 | 6 |

Figure 4-1. Offensive and Defensive Mental Skill Survey

| | | | | | | | |
|---|---|---|---|---|---|---|---|
| 19. My mind _____ wanders to end results and I have trouble focusing on the process of playing well. | 0 | 1 | 2 | 3 | 4 | 5 | 6 |
| 20. I _____ mentally picture the game plan and how I will play before practice and games. | 0 | 1 | 2 | 3 | 4 | 5 | 6 |
| 21. I _____ consistently train at a high level of intensity. | 0 | 1 | 2 | 3 | 4 | 5 | 6 |
| 22. I _____ find myself "going through the motions" in training sessions. | 0 | 1 | 2 | 3 | 4 | 5 | 6 |
| 23. I _____ focus well in practice/games when I have problems in my life outside of soccer. | 0 | 1 | 2 | 3 | 4 | 5 | 6 |
| 24. When I practice, I _____ have a specific purpose or goal to accomplish. | 0 | 1 | 2 | 3 | 4 | 5 | 6 |
| 25. I _____ have a high-energy walk between games (especially when I am tired or frustrated with the past game). | 0 | 1 | 2 | 3 | 4 | 5 | 6 |
| 26. Observers can _____ tell from my body language that I made a mistake or am playing poorly. | 0 | 1 | 2 | 3 | 4 | 5 | 6 |
| 27. My coaches and teammates can _____ tell by my body language and behaviors that I am frustrated and upset. | 0 | 1 | 2 | 3 | 4 | 5 | 6 |
| 28. If I am having difficulty with my play, I _____ take it out on my teammates or coaches. | 0 | 1 | 2 | 3 | 4 | 5 | 6 |

**SCORING**: To determine your mental skill strengths and weaknesses, use the following scoring method *by section*. REVERSE score the following items: 3, 5, 7, 10, 18, 20, 21, 23, 24, 25 as follows: 0=6; 1=5; 2=4; 3=3; 4=2; 5=1; 6=0

> • If the score is *8 or fewer points*, this area is a mental strength.
>
> • If the score is between *9 and 12 points*, you appear to have some difficulty with the particular mental skills; some work is recommended
>
> • If the score is between *13 and 24 points*, you appear to have more serious difficulty with this particular mental skill; more work is definitely needed before your performance suffers more.

**Defensive Mental Skills:**

Section 1 = questions 1–4 deal with the ability to refocus and recover upon adversity (mistakes, setbacks).

Section 2 = questions 5–8 refer to confidence level.

Section 3 = questions 9–12 have to do with the ability to control levels of "intensity" (level of anxiety/muscle tension).

**Offensive Mental Skills:**

Section 4 = questions 13–16 refer to the ability to stay focused with distractions present.

Section 5 = questions 17–20 inquire about your ability to prepare physically/mentally for practice and matches.

Section 6 = questions 21–24 deal w/ the quality of training

Section 7 = questions 25–28 refer to your physical presentation when faced with adversity

Section 1 = _____; Section 2 = _____; Section 3 = _____; Section 4 = _____; Section 5 = _____; Section 6 = _____; Section 7 = _____.

Figure 4-1. Offensive and Defensive Mental Skill Survey (cont.)

• Emotional and energy control—the ability to remain composed under pressure, and be energized and motivated in practice settings or when playing against lesser opponents

Having each player complete this survey will provide both coaches and players with some important information. For example, if a player has higher scores (which represent weaknesses), it indicates deficiencies in the specific mental skill, which should then become a priority. If a player has high numbers on all of the offensive mental skills, then this player is failing to dominate his performance, via a lack of confidence and trust in his abilities and skills, while high scores on the defensive mental skills indicate problems with adversity and emotionality. Other players may have weaknesses across both types of mental skills. Helping players interpret their scores on the Offensive and Defensive Mental Skills Survey and relate them to their present actions on the field can be a very valuable learning exercise for both coaches and players. Players can self-diagnose the issues leading to inconsistent performances, and coaches will be better informed about the specific performance barriers limiting each player's performance potentials. Chapters 5 and 6 outline and detail these performance barriers.

Courtesy of UMASS Sports Information

Figure 4-2. Players who have sound offensive and defensive mental skills dominate their performances and remain focused under adversity.

# Chapter Summary

- Two critical areas of optimal performance that are seldom trained are the mental and emotional toughness skills.
- Mental and emotional skills can be organized into offensive and defensive skill categories.
- Offensive skills allow players to perform at the top of their games, while defensive skills enable players to remain composed in the face of adversity.
- Offensive mental skills include confidence, competitive focus, preparation and readiness, using productive images, and quality training.
- Defensive mental skills include refocus, recovery, intensity control, physical presentation, and emotional/energy control.

# Section II:
# Barriers and Breakdowns to Performance Excellence

# 5

# Barriers to Top Performance I: Physical, Technical, and Tactical Barriers

This chapter details the many physical, technical, and tactical barriers to optimizing performance, while Chapter 6 outlines the team, mental, emotional, and inspirational barriers. Remember, when players master their technical and mental mechanics, as well as their mental toughness, automaticity of execution should result on a consistent basis. They should be better able to execute well-learned plays in pressure situations without thinking about the mechanical aspects of the chosen skill. The important word in the two previous sentences is "should." The practicality of teaching and training dictates that the more you practice something, the better it should be performed. But anyone involved in soccer knows that is not always the case. Why? Experts in the motor learning field have reported that physical, technical, and mental skills are susceptible to short-term conditions, such as fatigue, inadequate hydration and nutrition, mood swings, and external and internal distractions that result from the numerous variables that interfere with skill execution (Schmidt & Wrisberg, 2000).

These interference variables, referred to as *performance barriers,* have the capability of interfering with attempts at maximizing efforts and execution (Figure 5-1). The performance barriers covered in this chapter range from the physical (e.g., not fit enough) and technical (e.g., weak at keeping ball possession), to the tactical (e.g., not understanding tactical positional demands) aspects of play.

| Technical-Tactical Barriers | Physical Barriers |
|---|---|
| • Role ambiguity | • Poor sleep habits |
| • Lack of understanding of the game plan | • Lack of proper recovery and hydrating |
| • Too much focus on execution of tactics | |
| • Game-speed training | • Lack of proper fueling |
| • Visualization of roles and game plan | • Training fatigue |
| | • Poor fitness conditioning |

Figure 5-1. Common performance barriers

The first steps in combating these barriers are to be aware of their existence and recognize when they directly or indirectly affect performance. What you may think is at the root of a performance problem may not be the case at all. Teams and players who under-perform, or are inconsistent, may be coping with "all of the above" barriers, which range from the physical to the inspirational. Determine whether the performance problem is primarily due to physical, technical, or tactical difficulties, because these areas are the easiest to "fix." For example, training smarter, improving technical execution via quality reps, or watching more video are methods players could utilize. Another example is if a team is losing leads toward the end of games. It may not be that they are losing confidence or motivation to perform, signifying mental reasons. It may simply be that the players are physically fatigued due to the heat or being on the pitch for extended periods of time. When players are fatigued, skill execution can break down, causing ineffective plays and mental errors. This situation could also be due to players who are "running on empty" in terms of inadequate hydration or nutrition.

Performance difficulties due to mental, team, emotional, or inspirational issues are much more complex, which is why coaches should rule out physical, technical, or tactical reasons first. Another method of defeating these potential performance barriers is to challenge players to expand their individual capacities. Players must determine which areas of their performances are strengths and which are weaknesses, and they must decide on their own to strive toward maximizing their performance potential. Coaches are critical in this reflective process. The following sections detail the myriad physical, technical, and tactical barriers that could be contributing to individual player- and team-performance difficulties, or simply not playing to potential.

# Physical Barriers

Physical barriers are the easiest barriers to overcome, which is why athletes must constantly work to improve upon all areas of game-related fitness. Although some barriers may appear to be "little things," inadequate nutrition and hydration can unquestionably interfere with top performance—as much as not having the physical skills necessary to compete. These two variables contribute greatly to the amount of energy that players bring to the practice and game fields. The basic fitness principles at the core of a player's execution potential include strength, power, aerobic fitness, anaerobic conditioning, agility, coordination, and speed/quickness. Although some of these attributes are "gifts," those not blessed with this type of natural talent can still maximize what they do have.

Most people know what can happen when the wrong type of fuel is added to their cars. The car may begin with some "pinging," then move on to "chugging," a decrease in pick-up and performance, then finally a complete shutdown of all operations. This often-used analogy paints a clear picture of what occurs in athletes' bodies when poor nutrition is practiced on a consistent basis. Soccer players, in their strength and conditioning work and on the practice and game fields, are in dire need of energy that can only be provided via the food and fluids ingested.

Figure 5-2. To maximize the efficiency of strength and conditioning training, players must be optimally energized and hydrated.

Carbohydrates are a prime energy source for high-intensity activity (e.g., conditioning, short bursts of speed and power), fats are necessary and provide energy for longer-duration activities (e.g., cardiovascular activities), and protein is a building block for tissue growth. Are players taking in adequate amounts of these prime nutrients, as well as the essential vitamins and minerals? Each of the essential vitamins and minerals carries out a different function in the body. Specific references are presented in Section III that offer greater detail about the relationship between sound nutrition and optimal sport performance.

The importance of keeping the body hydrated cannot be overemphasized. Ensuring that players are adequately hydrated before, during, and after competing should be a standard carried out daily. Insufficient hydration will not only have a deleterious affect on performance, but may also lead to more serious health consequences, even death (Baechle & Earle, 2000). After workouts, practices, and games, the rule of thumb is to replenish fluids at a rate of one pint for every pound of body weight lost.

Another important physical barrier in need of attention is a lack of flexibility in joints, ligaments, tendons, and muscles. By performing dynamic stretches before, but especially after, practices and games, athletes will greatly reduce nagging injuries and muscle pulls, and improve muscle recovery while decreasing delayed onset muscle soreness. Dynamic stretching entails sport-specific stretches that mimic the actions that players will use during practice and games. Static stretching (i.e., a slow stretch and hold for a count of 15 to 30 seconds) is still utilized and is conducive to enhancing flexibility while decreasing the chance of injury. The majority of players, knowing full well the benefits of stretching, still go through the motions while they stretch.

Ensuring adequate sleep prior to practice days and games is another "little thing" that can make a difference between playing well and hoping for another chance. It is commonly accepted that each individual has a set number of sleep hours that works best for them. Knowing what this set number is and making it a priority to get the needed rest is the important next step for any athlete. Another important point derived from research is that drinking alcohol and caffeinated drinks can interfere with the sleep process. What is injected into the body's systems can definitely have positive and negative impacts on not only sleep, but also performance.

# Technical/Tactical Barriers

Coaches devote most (if not all) of their time during practice sessions to technical and tactical execution. It is the aim of this book for coaches to see how they can devote more time to the mental aspects of performance, while also maximizing the time given to physical and technical/tactical coaching. Applying mental-training principles during practice can maximize the quality of players' execution and improve coaching effectiveness. Most coaches would be surprised to know the many ways that they already incorporate mental-skills training into their coaching practices (refer to Chapter 11 for more on this topic).

Technical and tactical coaching involves the teaching of technical mechanics and reinforcing sound performance cues, in addition to the teaching of offensive and defensive schemes. Barriers exist when players do not adequately internalize these teachings (technical execution and strategical plays), and therefore are unable to apply them during "game-speed" simulations or actual games. If players do not see how these individual drill segments fit into the big picture of the game, the chances of them applying the skills in pressure situations are quite low. Since "knowledge is power," sharing with players the myriad technical mechanics involved with successful skill execution is critical. Again, these technical mechanics range from the locomotor component, to sensory, conceptual, and strategical elements.

Practicing sound mechanics in game-simulated repetitions leads to automatic skill execution, echoing the importance of performing simulated practice drills and improving upon the quality of practice. Players who are allowed to "go through the motions" during practice are not adequately prepared to play and will fail to fulfill their roles or offer consistent contributions to the team effort. Players must not only see how

Figure 5-3. To be able to play at the highest level, players must maximize the quality of their physical and technical training.

training applies to their specific roles during the game, but also how they can practice at a speed that matches game conditions. Practicing in this manner takes the synergy of both players and coaches. For example, players must apply what is done in practice on the game field, as well as practice with game-time intensity. In addition, coaches must design practices that are game-simulated and competitive in nature, while also helping players apply the training principles learned in practice on the game field. Improving upon the quality of practice requires both parties working toward the same ideal—improved game performance. Much more is said about improving upon the quality of individual and team practice in Chapter 15.

# Chapter Summary

- Physical, technical, and mental skills are susceptible to short-term conditions, due to the numerous variables—called performance barriers—that interfere with skill execution.
- Coaches should determine whether a performance problem is primarily due to physical, technical, or tactical difficulties first, because these issues are the easiest to fix.
- Performance difficulties due to mental, team, emotional, or inspirational issues are much more complex, which is why coaches should rule out physical, technical, and tactical reasons first.
- Inadequate nutrition and hydration can unquestionably interfere with top performance, as much as not having the physical skills necessary to compete at the respective level.
- Applying mental-training principles during practice can maximize the quality of players' execution and improve coaching effectiveness.
- Technical and tactical barriers exist when players do not adequately internalize these teachings, and therefore are unable to apply them during "game-speed" simulations during practice sessions and again come game time.

# 6

# Barriers to Top Performance II: Team, Mental, Emotional, and Inspirational Barriers

Obstacles that can greatly impact optimal performance include team barriers (e.g., little trust within the team), mental barriers (e.g., confidence level not consistent enough), emotional barriers (e.g., resistant to change), and inspirational barriers (e.g., lack of drive and commitment) (Figure 6-1). Chapter 5 addressed the most salient physical, technical, and tactical barriers to consistent, optimal performance.

## Team Barriers

Team barriers include those variables that can interfere with players maximizing their contributions toward a collective team effort. The term "team" is used in this context to represent the entirety of all team members, but could be adapted to include positional units, such as the backs, midfielders, and strikers.

Asking the following team-related questions helps to identify potential team barrier "hotspots":

- Does the team play consistent enough to make a run at the conference title each season?
- Does the team play to the level of competition (i.e., play well when facing the elite, but not as well when facing underdogs)?
- How unified is the team?

| Emotional Barriers | Inspirational Barriers |
|---|---|
| • Low stress tolerance | • Disconnection between actions and beliefs |
| • Poor coping with time demands and frustrations | • Lack of true commitment |
| • Lack of social support | • Lack of honest effort |
| • Lack of trust in others | • Lack of purpose and passion |
| • Dissatisfaction, worry over uncontrollables | |
| • Lack of resiliency | Team Barriers |
| | • Unwilling to sacrifice for team |
| Mental Barriers | • Deciding to "go through the motions" during practices |
| • Poor mental recovery | • Inability to challenge teammates |
| • Poor/lack of coping with stress | • Does not consistently achieve preset standards |
| • Lack of self-confidence | • Unwilling to commit to team's goals and identity |
| • Irrational thinking | • Poor communication |
| • Excuse-making | • Inability to hold each other accountable |
| • Poor concentration | • Limited amount of trust |
| • Poor problem solving skills | • Unwilling to ask for help |
| • Lack of awareness (what works and what doesn't) | |
| • Fear of failure/mistakes | |
| • Fear of disappointing others | |

Figure 6-1. Team, mental, emotional, and inspirational performance barriers

- Are players only partially committed to the team's pursuits?
- Do players understand and accept their roles?
- Do players blame each other when adversity hits, or do they pull together and get past it?
- Do players help lead the team through their communication and actions?
- Overall, does the team hope to win or expect to win?
- How is the team leadership? Who leads the team (other than coaches)?
- How does the team treat reserve players?
- Are teammates able to challenge each other?
- What is the percentage of practice sessions that could be classified as quality, productive sessions?
- How much trust exists within this team?

These questions bring to light the most salient team barriers facing most soccer teams. As Figure 6-1 shows, these barriers include a lack of commitment to team objectives, little to no sacrifice for the sake of the team effort, poor communication and compatibility, lack of acceptance of roles, training of inconsistent quality, little team trust

Courtesy of USC Sports Information

Figure 6-2. For teams to be truly cohesive, they must be able to successfully overcome team barriers.

and leadership, and a lack of accountability. The first step in building effective teams is to identify the most salient problem areas inhibiting the process (or those things that could become barriers). These questions help coaches target these specific areas for intervention. The next step is for coaches to intervene with proven strategies that will break through these team barriers (i.e., team-building and communication interventions), which are detailed in Chapter 10.

# Mental Barriers

Going "beyond the X's & O's" entails an awareness of the existence of barriers and the knowledge of skill strategies to overcome them. Having your players complete the Offensive and Defensive Mental Skill Survey in Chapter 4 will help them gain a better awareness of the specific mental and emotional barriers currently interfering with automatic and consistent execution. Common mental barriers, as Figure 6-1 indicates, include debilitating thoughts and self-talk, inadequate concentration and refocusing, poor confidence, inadequate preparation, fear of failure, poor coping response to stress/adversity, and unrealistic expectations. All of these barriers have the potential to influence technical and mechanical execution and performance, because of the interference each causes in the players' heads. Remind players of the importance of trusting their talent, skills, mental toughness, and training prior to competing. Unproductive mental activity occurs when a lack of trust exists.

To be more specific, mental interference refers to any mental activity that interferes with the automatic execution of a well-learned skill—also referred to as mental mechanics. This unproductive mental activity involves the following elements:

- Negative thoughts, such as "I hope I don't give the ball away again."
- Being analytical too close to execution (paralysis by overanalysis)
- Self-defeating self-talk, such as "I can't slow down the winger. She is so fast."
- Thinking about a past event, such as "The last time we played here I had a nightmare."
- Worrying over an event in the foreseeable future, such "What if I mishandle the next crossed ball?"
- Making excuses for failures, mistakes, and even successes
- Fear of making mistakes, fear of failure, fear of injury, fear of letting others down, or worrying about being embarrassed

How often do players think this way? When they have had bad performances, how much of their thinking was of this type? In most cases, when players perform well, their minds are either free from this clutter or they think productively about performance-related cues or confidence-building thoughts or self-talk.

# Emotional Barriers

*To discuss the mental aspects of the game, we must also address the emotional and spiritual sides."*
—Pete Waite, Head Volleyball Coach, Wisconsin, (2002, p. 304)

As Figure 6-1 indicates, the emotional barriers that can adversely affect technical execution and performance include insufficient intensity control, social disconnection, fear of failing, lack of resiliency to stressors, and a lack of trust in personal skills and training. Emotional barriers such as these affect each athlete differently. Some athletes respond better in the heat of battle when they are emotionally charged up, even exhibiting anger and frustration toward their opponent, while others play better when they are more composed. Some coaches love to give the big rallying pep talks to pump up the troops, which may work for a couple of players, but in the sport of soccer, players need to think and react fast on their feet. In general, the majority of players do not play their best if they are too emotionally charged up. The key is to realize what works for each athlete.

Incidents can happen if athletes do not keep a lid on their emotions. A good example from Major League Baseball came during game three of the 2003 American League Playoffs. Boston Red Sox pitcher Pedro Martinez allegedly beaned a New York Yankee batter, which led to greater frustrations between the two teams. Roger Clemens then threw a brushback pitch to a Red Sox batter, which caused the benches to clear, even prompting a 72-year-old Yankee coach, Don Zimmer, to throw a punch at Martinez. Later in the game, a Yankee pitcher allegedly punched a Red Sox groundskeeper.

Commentator Peter Gammons stated that this game was an "embarrassing game" for the two teams and for baseball. This incident is only one example—how many more examples happen each week in college or professional sports?

Examples such as these illustrate how a lack of emotional control can affect how players bounce back after setbacks during play. Some players have low stress tolerance, so when pressure begins to pile up, combined with additional adversity, such as mistakes or important plays, they are too frustrated to keep their minds on performance-related cues, which leads to missed passes, lost goal-scoring chances, and bad fouls. Some players do not have coping routines to help them deal with times of stress and adversity, so as stress increases, muscle tension and/or negative thoughts also increase, leading to more mechanical mistakes and, eventually, a total lapse in performance. Chapter 12 details strategies that can be used to overcome these barriers.

## Inspirational Barriers

A lack of inspiration is related to why someone plays a particular sport and what makes him happiest while playing. Athletes play sports for hundreds of reasons. Do you know why your players play soccer? What are they getting out of the experience? Very often, players' motives for playing are incongruent with their coaches' motives. Players who are not having their primary motives met are less driven to work toward their coaches' motives (better play, wins, championships), are not as satisfied with the experience, and may not try as hard or play as well.

Courtesy of USC Sports Information

Figure 6-3. Top players are driven by intrinsic factors and aspirations.

Asking players what their primary motives are for playing, as well as what their future aspirations are in soccer, will help coaches gain access to players' inner drives and motivations. Then, coaches can help to meet the players' primary motives, which, in turn, may encourage players to begin to adopt the coaches' primary motives. Coaches primarily want their teams to improve, practice hard, and get results. Players' primary motives could range from wanting to improve their games to just being affiliated with the team. Most coaches just assume that players share their motives, which in most cases is simply not true. Figure 6-1 outlines additional barriers to consider, including a lack of purpose, satisfaction, and enjoyment in sporting endeavors.

# Chapter Summary

- Team barriers include those variables that can interfere with players maximizing their contributions to a collective team effort.
- Common team barriers include a lack of commitment to team objectives, little to no sacrifice for the sake of the team effort, poor communication, lack of acceptance of roles, training of inconsistent quality, and little team trust.
- Common mental barriers include debilitating thoughts and self-talk, inadequate concentration and refocusing, poor confidence, inadequate preparation, fear of failure, and poor coping response to stress and adversity.
- Mental interference refers to any mental activity that interferes with the automatic execution of a well-learned skill, which is also referred to as mental mechanics.
- Emotional barriers that can adversely affect technical execution and performance include insufficient intensity control, social disconnection, lack of resiliency to stressors, and a lack of trust in personal skills and training.
- Asking players what their primary motives are for playing, as well as what their future aspirations are in soccer, will help coaches gain access to players' inner drives and current motivations.
- Figures 5-1 and 6-1 list the most salient performance barriers. When players or teams are hitting rough performance spells, coaches can read through these lists of performance barriers and, through a process of elimination, come to the root of the problems. Remember, coaches should begin with the easiest barriers to fix (i.e., physical, technical, tactical), and then proceed to the more complex areas, if needed.

# 7

# Technical and Mental Mechanical Breakdowns in Execution

Previous chapters detailed the many types of factors that could adversely affect performance at any time. This chapter goes into greater detail on how these barriers interfere with the mechanical execution of passing, dribbling, shooting, blocking shots, and making plays.

Consistent and successful skill execution requires three interactive processes (Schmidt and Wrisberg, 2000). Performance barriers can interfere with each one of the following processes:

- Mental mechanics include accurate analysis of required information—namely, specific cues picked up from what is seen and heard prior to ball reception. This analysis is followed by the appropriate selection of movement patterns based on the motor program already established through quality repetitions in training and game experience.
- Mental toughness is defined as a proficiency at being able to produce productive mental states, including confidence, optimal concentration, intensity, readiness, and composed thinking and feeling during stressful times.
- Automaticity of performance involves being able to be consciously free from performance barriers. Not only do these barriers interfere with the ability to "let go" and allow talent, skill, and training to take over (trust), but they also limit performance by interfering with mechanical efficiency via breakdowns in *information processing* and *sequencing* (Moore, 1998).

# Information Processing Breakdowns

## Jamming

Figure 7-1 depicts how errors in mechanical execution, namely informational processing and sequencing problems, affect performance. Fundamentally, information-processing errors occur due to excessive thinking. Bill Moore (1998), a researcher and practitioner, has referred to these errors as *jamming*. When an athlete gets "jammed," valuable information that is needed for the current play is being missed because of too much "static," which refers to too much thinking about the wrong things. Static occurs when players overanalyze the next play ("I get so confused with the opponents' zonal marking"), being too apprehensive ("The opponent's attack is so fast"), or by second-guessing ("I hope I can work through the congestion to get to the crosses"). Static then takes up room in the player's limited attentional capacity, taking away from the important environmental cues necessary for successful execution, including the

---

**Information Processing Breakdowns**
*Jamming*
- mechanical cause/consequence = change in technical mechanics (passing, striking, dribbling, ball control)
- mental cause/consequence = excessive mental activity (static); unable to switch attention
- performance cause/consequence = overanalyze performance situations; mental errors; execution errors

**Sequencing Breakdowns**
*Aiming*
- mechanical = change in mechanics
- mental = fearful of missing the primary target, and fearful of the outcome of the play
- performance = excess tension not needed or desired

*Pressing*
- mechanical = change in mechanics
- mental = too outcome-oriented; unrealistic expectation of success (one out of 10 chance of getting it there)
- performance = increase in tension, which leads to a decrease in movement and technical accuracy; inaccuracy; passing-striking-receiving errors

*Controlling*
- mechanical = ineffective movements; change in mechanics
- mental = fearful of missing the target; fearful of outcome
- performance = inaccurate passes, shots-saves; errors

---

Figure 7-1. Mechanical breakdowns: Information processing and sequencing errors

defensive/offensive positioning of teammates and opponents, communication on the field, and coaching points from the bench and during breaks. Other forms of "static" include negative thinking, thinking too much on the outcome and not on the process of execution, and inappropriate attentional focus, such as being too narrow, too broad, too external, or too internal in their focus.

Jamming can adversely affect all positional players. Players can get caught being too narrow and internal in their focus, meaning that they are only thinking about their specific assignment (limited cues) on a particular play, regardless of what could be happening around them. If they are thinking in this manner, they may miss key information and be left ill-prepared for the adjusted play (e.g., overlapping runs, mismatches on defensive assignments). Again, being too much "in the head" limits the amount of intuitiveness and reactionary playmaking. All players must be able to adjust at a moment's notice or they will be left in the dark, or on the bench. Other difficulties could arise from being too broad and external in focus, which is discussed further in Chapter 12. Briefly, players who are too broad in focus attempt to internalize too many cues around them, some of which may be of little to no help to them. Likewise, being too external means that players are focusing on their environment too much, rather than thinking about what they need to do to make their next touch productive.

# Sequencing Breakdowns

According to Moore (1998), sequencing errors do not occur as a result of inaccurate information, but rather are due to incorrect movement execution stemming from mental interference. Such breakdowns consist of aiming, pressing, and controlling.

### Aiming

When strikers or goalkeepers are caught aiming a shot or distribution, it means that they have an excessive concern for the target, such as the upper corner for a shot or a striker's head on a dropkick. Once players attempt to overly control their passes, shots, or kicks, a slight change in mechanical execution usually occurs, so passes that are usually on target are either overpassed (weighted too heavily) or off-target. For example, ball strikers, especially those who place an overemphasis on the specific target, get caught changing their mechanics just enough to potentially alter the flight of the ball. Although a particular spot on goal or in the box is the ultimate target, some players can get so narrow in their focus that they dismiss some important execution cues (e.g., squaring hips, trajectory, and ball contact).

### Pressing

Mechanics can also be altered when players, for example, try too hard on a pass, such as by trying to force a pass to a specific spot from a difficult body position or location on the field. This situation requires adding more weight to the pass or chip, adding muscle tension and changing movement sequencing. This action is referred to as pressing and can also be seen with keepers who attempt to box a crossed ball down the field and fail to get good contact on the ball. Additionally, shooters are guilty of pressing when they try to strike the ball too hard, thus changing their usual mechanics. Common sense would indicate that putting more force into a pass or shot would improve the play, but if this force is not the usual pace, the mechanics will be changed, thereby altering the trajectory and direction of the ball. Trying to press in this fashion may turn a would-be highlight save or shot into a highlight miss, because the automatic, reactionary action was forced, thus changing the movement.

## Controlling

One controlling scenario entails a wide player who is fearful of striking another crossed ball either into the hands of the keeper or another cross out-of-bounds, and therefore attempts to exert too much control over the strike. This controlled strike results from excessive worry over the presumed outcome of the play, practicing future-oriented thinking ("What if I miss?"), instead of just swinging the leg with a process- and present-oriented style of thinking. Similarly, the mechanical execution of this controlled strike is changed somewhat, leading to what the flanker feared prior to the cross: another unproductive service!

Courtesy of Dartmouth Sports Information

Figure 7-2. Successful players are able to combat mechanical breakdowns like jamming, aiming, pressing, or controlling.

Courtesy of Vanderbilt University Sports Information

Figure 7-3. Maximizing the learning experience entails knowing the root causes of execution errors.

Midfielders who worry about the outcome of their next pass, or cannot seem to let go of an errant pass, will probably repeat the mistake due to overcontrolling the passing mechanics or having too narrow a focus, and thus fail to see the limited space and time around the ball. Defenders who are fearful of another missed tackle, or of allowing a striker to turn them, will also try to overcontrol the execution. Keepers who attempt to overcontrol the throw or punt will also change their mechanics, thus mishitting and sending the ball out of bounds or straight up in the air and onto the foot of an opposing striker.

What percentages of players' mistakes are due to these specific mental mechanical breakdowns? Coaches should discuss this very important question with their players. Assisting players in acknowledging the causes of their mistakes can give them valuable information on how to correct these mechanical errors. The chapters contained in Section III specify training strategies that players can practice to effectively combat information and sequencing errors so that they can not only sharpen their mental mechanics, but also automatically execute the skills needed at game time.

# Chapter Summary

- Consistent and successful skill execution requires the interactive processes of mental mechanics, mental toughness, and automaticity of performance.
- Performance barriers interfere with the ability of players to "let go" and allow their talent, skill, and training to take over, but they also limit performance by interfering with mechanical efficiency via informational processing and sequencing breakdowns.
- When a player gets "jammed," valuable information that is needed for the current play is being missed because of too much "static."
- When strikers are caught aiming shots, it means that they have an excessive concern for a target instead of just getting good ball contact and striking the ball past the goalkeeper. When players attempt to overly control their execution, a change in mechanical execution usually takes place.
- Attacking players are sometimes guilty of pressing when they try to strike the ball too hard, thus changing their usual mechanics.
- Players who worry about the outcome of the upcoming play, or cannot seem to let go of a past missed play, will probably repeat the mistake(s) due to overcontrolling their mechanics.

# Section III:
# Training Strategies for
# Automatic Execution

# 8

# Training for Automaticity I: Combating Physical and Technical-Tactical Barriers

## Physical Strength and Conditioning: Physical Toughness

Volumes of resources exist that address the many aspects of physical toughness, including cardiovascular training, agility training, flexibility training, speed training, resistance training, plyometric training, and sport-specific conditioning (Baechle & Earl, 2000; Emma, 2003; McKown & Malone, 2003). A thorough review of these training protocols is beyond the scope of this book, but some fundamental recommendations have been posited to help coaches and athletes combat the most salient physical barrier—not being fit, fast, or strong enough to maximize performance potential. These recommendations have been encapsulated into a "top 10" list of sport science tips, similar to one published by Matt Fitzgerald (2003).

**The Top 10 Sport Science Tips**

*Tip #1: Periodization of Training*

Periodization is the process of increasing training stress while inducing lowered frequencies and/or intensities of workload in time for optimal recovery and ultimately increased performance (Baechle, Earle, & Wathen, 2000; Bompa, 1983; Loehr, 1994). In the off-season, a priority is given to resistance training (hypertrophy, strength, and power), and in the preseason the priority shifts to both sport practice and sport-specific movements. An additional priority is establishing team unity and mental toughness. The remaining chapters of this book will help with this endeavor. The highest priority of in-season training is sport practice and game execution, with attention given to the maintenance of the conditioning program, team building, and mental toughness training. Coaches should plan their seasons in this manner to maximize their players' and team's potential. Some coaches attempt to do too much conditioning during the competitive season (following the "more is better" motto), which acts to fatigue the players when they should be recovering and getting reenergized.

*Tip #2: Intensity of Training*

Training intensity is considered a key variable to enhanced physical performance, whether it be striving to improve upon speed, strength, endurance, or power. Another term used to describe training intensity is training stress. Later in this chapter, more information is provided regarding the proper implementation of training stress, leading to overload and enhanced performance. It is very important for coaches to be careful in how they program intensity or stress levels to their athletes. Too little stress will result in underperforming and underachieving, while too much stress could result in training stress syndromes such as distress, staleness, or burnout. The science of maximizing potential should lead coaches to adopt the attitude of "training smarter," instead of simply "training longer."

*Tip #3: Progressive Overload Principles*

As with training stress, the body adapts best to training regimens that gradually increase intensity/stress levels. Progressive overload applies not only to lifting greater volumes (more weight and more sets), but also longer running distances, more sprint repetitions, or additional sets of plyometric training exercises. Ensuring a progression in introducing greater loads and volume will not only maximize gains (in cardiovascular fitness, speed, agility, strength, or power), but will also do so in a safe manner. The "old-school" approach to preseason training should be avoided—the days when players limped from drill to drill reeking of Ben Gay™ because their muscles were so sore and stiff. When players come into training already fit, their bodies will recover faster from practice to practice. Those players who come into training camp unfit will struggle to keep up, and may experience fatigue and soreness, but this situation should not be compounded by using fitness sessions as punishment, which will only serve to injure the player. As much as it will make coaches feel better, punishment running for unfit players is not smart training. More physical-toughness aspects of preseason training are mentioned later in this chapter.

*Tip #4: Principle of Specificity*

Coaches and athletes must realize that each position in soccer requires different training modalities based upon positional requirements. Also, each player differs in terms of the intensity levels that can be maintained and rest and recovery abilities. Specificity also refers to conditioning players in game-simulated exercises and position-specific movements. Positional requirements must be prioritized in the designing of strength and conditioning programs.

*Tip #5: Pretraining Evaluations*

A hint of caution for coaches and strength coaches on the importance of evaluating fitness and strength levels prior to specific conditioning programming: Due to specificity and progression concerns, players should be assessed prior to beginning any conditioning and fitness-training programs. Having a sense of each player's baseline measures of strength, speed, power, vertical, and endurance is invaluable when designing specific areas of programming. Physical characteristics, age level, playing and conditioning experience, and current health status are important characteristics that need serious consideration.

Ensuring that players know appropriate lifting techniques, safety concerns, and spotting methods is critical before embarking on a program. Before plyometric training, in particular, numerous assessments should be conducted. For example, players should be able to hold a half-squat position for 30 seconds without falling prior to performing plyometric exercises (Potachu & Chu, 2000). For plyometric strength exercises, players should be able to squat a one-repetition maximum that is 1.5 times their body weight and bench press a one-repetition maximum that is 1.5 times their body weight or perform five clap push-ups. Other preassessment standards have been established for speed workouts as well (Baechle, Earle, & Wathen, 2000).

*Tip #6: Fueling the Machine*

Detailed information on eating for enhanced functioning and optimal performance is provided later in this chapter. Specific areas addressed include critical nutrients, the effects of hydration, the content of pre-event meals, and eating for optimal recovery.

*Tip #7: Recovery Training*

Athletes and coaches at the top levels of sport consider "recovery" to be an important aspect of training. Recovery stands for more than just resting outside of training. Recovery could include treatments, such as taking ice baths or whirlpools to help heal and restore sore muscles, or doing extra stretching and flexibility work after hard training sessions. Recovery can be passive, such as watching video, using imagery, or engaging in a favorite hobby. Recovery can also be active, such as cross-training, performing yoga, or incorporating lower-intensity workouts. Recovery training is not only important for physiological reasons, such as taxing other energy systems and muscle groups, but also for mental and emotional recovery. Taking time outside of the sport can really help to revitalize and restore energy and motivation.

## Tip #8: Hydration

Because athletes usually replace only two-thirds of the water that they lose through sweat, they put themselves at risk of dehydration and decreased performance. More information is provided about the importance of proper hydration later in this chapter.

## Tip #9: Dynamic Flexibility

Static stretching, whereby a stretch is held for 30 to 40 seconds, has been the most recommended form of active flexibility training for years, but dynamic stretching is gaining popularity. With this type of stretching, sport-specific movements are used that mimic the speed of specific movements used during play. Partner stretching has long been used to incorporate both passive and active stretching. This type of stretching, called proprioceptive neuromuscular facilitation (PNF), may be the best form of stretching, especially when combined with sport-specific, dynamic stretching, due to the three types of muscle actions utilized to elicit the stretch—namely the hold-relax-contract cycles. For example, instead of just bending over to stretch the hamstrings, a partner would hold the leg up in a 90-degree fashion (so that the stretched leg is parallel to the ground). After the player holds this stretch for 30 seconds, the partner lowers the leg just enough to relax the muscle. Then, for another 30 seconds, the partner will attempt (in a slow and deliberate manner) to raise the leg higher than the previous stretch position. After this step, the player will be told to lower the leg slowly while the partner is offering slight resistance, thus forcing the muscle to contract. As a note of caution, partner PNF stretching should only be conducted under the watchful eye of a trained coach, as injury can easily occur if the stretches are not done correctly.

## Tip #10: Quality Training and Conditioning.

Chapter 15 describes a model for improving the quality of practice that can be applied directly to soccer training and strength and conditioning training. This model is based upon viewing training sessions as dynamic processes involving responsibilities from both athletes and coaches. The four main aspects of the model include improving upon coach and athlete attitudes toward training, preparation practices, execution strategies, and quality-control methods postpractice.

## Off-Season Conditioning

For coaches to be able to effectively apply the top 10 sport science tips to their teams, players must come into the preseason with some semblance of physical conditioning.

Coaches continually stress the importance of off-season conditioning. These same coaches provide off-season conditioning programs that normally incorporate the following components: weight training, cardiovascular training, speed work, agility training, plyometrics, and flexibility training. Although the major objective of off-season conditioning is to prepare the body for the grueling stress of preseason/training camp, other prime benefits of an organized conditioning program exist. In addition to increasing physical toughness, forcing a player to work through and beyond their "comfort levels" on his own over the summer months will greatly elevate his mental and emotional toughness. Physical, mental, and emotional toughening involves increasing the capacity to endure stress. A leader in the field of toughness training defined "toughness" as "the ability to consistently perform toward the upper range of your talent and skill regardless of competitive circumstances" (Loehr, 1994, p. 18).

If players give maximal effort to their physical conditioning and play during the off-season, they will experience increased gains in their physical, mental, and emotional toughness. Yet if a less-than-maximal effort is given during their off-season preparation and conditioning, numerous consequences will occur. Figure 8-1 details the many consequences that occur when athletes undertrain, or decide not to put in the effort and time necessary (Voight, 2000a). These consequences not only adversely affect the individual, but also the team. Consequences of coming into training camp undertrained could include negative effects on physiology, mental and emotional functioning, and skill training and performance.

The physical, mental, and emotional benefits of putting in maximal effort and time on the off-season conditioning/playing program are countless. Players who "cheat" their off-season conditioning can always be detected, especially if coaches recognize

| Physical Consequences | Mental Consequences |
| --- | --- |
| • major/minor pain | • poor concentration |
| • muscle soreness | • poor problem solving |
| • illness | • chronic mental fatigue |
| • decreased workrate | • mental mistakes |
| • lack of effort | • negative thinking |
| • incidence or continuance of injury | • decrease in confidence |
| • sleeping/eating problems | *Emotional Consequences* |
| • decrease in performance | • low motivation |
| *Skill Consequences* | • moodiness |
| • lack of quality | • anxiety |
| • less than full-speed | • nervousness |
| • rigid, clumsy performance | • lack of enjoyment |
| • going through the motions | • anger |
| • poor execution habits | • sadness |

Figure 8-1. Consequences of undertraining

the numerous symptoms mentioned in Figure 8-1, many of which will affect players' thinking, emotions, and physiology, as well as having team-wide consequences as training camp progresses. Recognizing those players who did not come into training camp ready is only the first step, with the next being figuring out how to deal with this inefficient preparation.

In general, coaches strategically design each training-camp session down to the last minute and the last play. When one or more players come into training camp ill-prepared, most coaches must make changes, often drastic changes, to these strategic plans. Instead of focusing primarily on certain technical or tactical aspects, coaches must spend more time than originally planned on fitness-related activities. Instead of being "ahead of the game" at the beginning of training camp, a team will begin the season behind the rest of the pack. When this situation occurs, it is important for coaches to avoid pushing their players too much, and instead attempt to get their players caught up on their fitness, as failure to do so can lead to injury and other consequences, including training stress syndromes, which are discussed later in this chapter. It is very important for coaches to continue to stress to their players the importance of "toughening up" in the off-season, or players will continually show up undertrained, thereby kick-starting the debilitating consequences, not only to themselves, but also to their teammates, the training camp experience, and potentially the success of the team throughout the season.

## Implementation of Training Stress

A final point about physical toughness is for coaches to be aware of the careful implementation of training stress. How many coaches know exactly how much to practice and how much to "push" their players physically and technically? To optimize peak performance, athletes, coaches, and strength coaches often adopt and reinforce accelerated training regimens. These changes usually take the form of large increments of training stress, longer training and conditioning sessions, and shorter recovery periods, all of which could prove detrimental to the individual's physical, psychological, and emotional standing.

The ESPN made-for-television movie, "The Junction Boys," showed Paul "Bear" Bryant's coaching methods during his first season at Texas A&M. The grueling practices during the hottest time of the day with little to no water were standard throughout his training camp. As it turned out, after waves of players left training camp in the wee hours of the morning, by the time the season came around his remaining players were so depleted and worn out that they finished the season with only two wins. Although this depicted an earlier era, the message taken from this movie—along with the many other stories about legendary coaching practices—is that knowing the difference between toughening players up and breaking them down is critical for their well-being and performance. With the help of sport science researchers, numerous training stress syndromes have been documented that can accompany inadequate training practices that range from overtraining, underrecovery, distress, staleness, and burnout.

For athletes to get fitter, stronger, and tougher mentally and emotionally, stress is required. According to Loehr (1994), for athletes to perform to their potential, they have to increase their ability to handle three kinds of stress—physical, emotional, and mental—and become stronger, more responsive, and more resilient to these stresses. Most sport and strength coaches at the elite levels realize that training stress needs to be carefully manipulated for optimal performance to occur. Careful adjustment of the level, intensity, and frequency of training stress is called training overload. After numerous bouts of overload, adaptation, and partial recovery, which could last for days or weeks, depending upon the sport and competitive schedule, a period of reduced training overload is induced, referred to as tapering. Tapering normally occurs days or weeks prior to important competitions, which allows the athletes' bodies to recover, compensate, and adapt to the periods of heavy training. Such a program adequately prepares athletes for maximal performances come game day. When athletes are unable to adapt to the overloading practice regimens or competitive stressors, negative adaptation results.

# Training Stress Syndromes

Negative adaptation occurs when any of these competitive stressors are heightened beyond an optimal point and continue over a period of time. The training stress syndrome is initiated by overtraining and underrecovery, and because of this excessive training stress without adequate rest, fatigue results, followed by the more debilitating syndromes of distress, staleness, and burnout.

## Overtraining and Underrecovery

Overtraining has been defined by Smith (1999) as an excessive overload of training stress without adequate rest or recovery from this stress, resulting in excessive fatigue, performance decrements, psychological/emotional disturbances, and an inability to train. An athlete who experiences these stages has coping systems that are progressively getting taxed, leading to the possibility of the athlete's adaptive mechanisms—both mental and physical—to be jeopardized. Athletes who continue to experience excessive training stress can regress from this overtrained stage into a distressed condition.

## Distress and Staleness

It is believed that distress is an acute response to being overtrained, which therefore can be treated by short-term interventions. If appropriate short-term interventions are not implemented at the distress stage, and if overtraining continues, athletes can regress further into the staleness syndrome, which is a serious manifestation of overtraining. Staleness is associated with numerous negative effects, especially behavioral, mental, emotional, and technical symptoms, as shown in Figure 8-2 (Voight, 2003). Distress and staleness are primarily caused by the physical and mental demands of increased training. Once stale, athletes who are exposed to greater increments of physical, mental, and emotional stress can begin exhibiting symptoms of burnout that represent a more severe reaction to overtraining.

*Technical Execution*
- monotonous practice sessions
- lack of quality execution
- loss of coordination
- poor communication with coaches
- confusion over role

*Workrate*
- decreased workrate
- going through the motions in practices/games
- affected by pain, soreness, and injury
- decreased power output

*Physiology*
- weight loss
- higher resting heart rate (HR)
- impeded respiration
- delayed return to normal HR
- increased muscle fatigue

*Mentality*
- mental fatigue
- lack of focus
- lack of motivation
- confused thinking
- poor problem solving
- negative thinking
- depression

*Emotionality*
- irritability
- moodiness
- boredom
- sadness
- anxiety
- lack of enjoyment
- negativism
- loss of self-esteem
- social withdrawal

Figure 8-2. Consequences of staleness due to overtraining/underrecovery

## Burnout

The major discriminating variable between staleness and burnout is that cognitive (mental) factors, such as a loss of interest and motivation, are reported to directly relate to burnout. Another distinguishing variable from the other phases of the training syndrome is that once athletes experience burnout, voluntary or involuntary withdrawal from sport can be inevitable (Silva, 1990). Generally, burnout is characterized by physical, mental, and emotional withdrawal from activities that once were sources of great satisfaction and enjoyment, but have been replaced by physical and psychological stress.

Successfully defeating the effects of distress and staleness in athletes can be accomplished via a multistage process. Intervention begins with gaining a better understanding of the causes of these training stress syndromes, over and above training volume, and the emotional, physical, and psychological stress experienced.

Numerous other factors have been found by Henschen (1986) to contribute to the debilitating effects of distress and staleness, including the length of the competitive season, training monotony, lack of positive reinforcement, abusiveness by coaches, stringent rules, high levels of competitive stress, perceived low accomplishment, and boredom.

One you are armed with these two important pieces of information—understanding the causes and recognizing the symptomology—appropriate intervention strategies can then be used to eliminate the debilitating effects of these syndromes and optimize athletes' methods of coping. Preventing fatigue and underrecovery, distress, and staleness takes great care and oversight from the entire coaching staff. Coaches who are more aware of the training stress syndromes and are diligent about monitoring their athletes' physiological, emotional, psychological, and performance functioning, are in better positions to eliminate or prevent the regressive continuance of the training stress syndrome. The intervention strategies can be categorized into three major areas: physical, mental, and performance-related interventions. These interventions, shown in Figure 8-3, are targeted for both players and coaches, as both are affected by the consequences of the training stress syndromes.

| *Physical* | *Mental* |
|---|---|
| • physical rest and recovery | • recovering mentally and emotionally |
| • energizing food | • setting short-term goals for practice |
| • periodization principles (tapering) | • self-challenges |
| • variety of training methods/exercises | • one-drill-at-a-time mentality |
| • incentives and rewards | • process-focused; improve on last |
| • competitions within training sessions | performance |
| • showers and massages | • energized thinking and self-talk |
| | • use of pre-practice routines |
| *Performance* | |
| • organized, competitive training sessions | • incorporating new drills |
| • reducing the monotony of practice (variety) | • asking for player input (favorite drills) |

Figure 8-3. Training stress syndrome interventions

The final aspect of effective interventions for eliminating staleness is continual feedback, reinforcement, and evaluation. Being aware of the potential causes, the signs and symptoms, and the primary goals of interventions represents a "three-pronged attack" on the deleterious effects of training stress syndromes. Intervention success can be subjectively and objectively evaluated once clear goals are made. Murphy (1996) identified numerous questions that can be asked to evaluate the effectiveness of staleness interventions, including the following:
- Are athletes performing better?
- Do the athletes feel better about their lives, performances, and fitness?

- How is their communication with teammates and coaches?
- Do athletes feel psychologically and emotionally stronger?
- Are athletes healthier and less injury-prone?
- Are athletes staying connected with their teammates?
- Do athletes feel adequately rested, recovered, and energized from practice session to practice session?
- Do athletes have adequate coping resources to deal with training stress?

Continually asking athletes these questions and obtaining their feedback regarding their physical, emotional, and psychological adjustments made to increased training stress is critical if coaches want to minimize training stress syndromes. Since increases in training stress, volume, and intensity will continue to be implemented by coaches and athletes who aspire for greatness, helping the athletes cope and adapt to these high training loads should be a primary concern for all involved, including athletes, coaches, strength coaches, sport psychologists, parents, and administrators. Educating all parties about training principles, causes and symptoms of training stress syndromes, and interventions designed to reduce or eliminate the effects of these syndromes, will go a long way to minimizing the number of athletes who unnecessarily suffer from distress, staleness, and burnout.

# Nutrition—Eating to Win

Most coaches appreciate the importance of eating nutritional foods prior to training and playing. But how many know what types of foods produce the most energy? How about the timing of eating prior to games? Not eating or hydrating properly can be a large performance barrier for any player. This section outlines the research-based recommendations regarding fueling up the "machine."

For peak athletic performance, the two primary dietary goals for most elite athletes are eating to maximize performance and eating for optimal body composition (Reimers & Ruud, 2000). According to the National Strength and Conditioning Association (NSCA), the best diets for performance enhancement are those that are individualized. What works for one athlete may not work for another. Individualized diets for soccer players should adhere to accepted guidelines. All athletes should:

- Monitor appropriate calorie intake. For example, general daily caloric intake guidelines, by height, for active athletes aged 17 to 23 are as follows (USC, 2003):
  - ✓ 5'7" and 5'8" = 2900
  - ✓ 5'10" = 3200
  - ✓ 6'0" = 3400
  - ✓ 5'9" = 3100
  - ✓ 5'11" = 3300
  - ✓ 6'1" = 3500
- Consume appropriate nutrient levels to prevent deficiencies.
- Follow diets containing recommended servings per food group.

- Avoid omitting food groups, since doing so can lead to deficiencies in specific nutrients.
- Consume significant amounts of the macronutrients, namely, proteins (20 percent of calories), carbohydrates (60 percent of calories), and lipids (less than 30 percent of calories).
- Avoid no-fat or low-fat diets, because these diets lead to deficiencies in key nutrients.
- Consume adequate amounts of vitamins and minerals in the diet.
- Gain weight safely (one to two pounds a week), by consuming 350 to 750 calories above daily requirements and eating five high-calorie meals.
- Lose weight safely (one to two pounds a week), by eating no less than 2000 calories a day (could be more) and eating nutritionally balanced, varied meals five times a day.
- Use pregame meals to properly hydrate and energize for peak performance.

The pre-event meal can do more to hinder than enhance performance. The purpose of the pregame meal is to maximize glycogen stores, or energy, minimize digestion during competition, provide fluids, and avoid gastric distress. Numerous factors must be taken into consideration when planning this meal, such as general dietary patterns and foods normally eaten by players (the pregame meal is not the time to introduce players to exotic foods), timing of the meal, specific components to the meal, and specific foods to be included. Include fluids in the meal, especially water and sport drinks, and offer nothing caffeinated, as caffeine is a diuretic and takes water out of the body.

The pregame meal should be eaten three-and-a-half to four hours prior to competition. This timing allows the stomach to be relatively empty at game time. In addition, the meal should consist mainly of complex carbohydrates, such as pastas, grains, vegetables, rice, and beans. Muscle carbohydrate (glycogen) depletion impairs performance. Carbohydrate-rich foods replenish this much-needed muscle carbohydrate. Simply put, carbohydrates are converted into blood sugar (glucose), which muscles burn for energy; any unused glucose gets stored in muscles and the liver as glycogen for future energy. Glycogen is the preferred fuel, because it is easier to burn than fat and is more readily available to the muscles. When the muscle glycogen gets depleted, blood glucose is required, and it is very difficult to maintain energy levels during extended play with glucose as the energy source (Roberts, 2001).

The meal should also include protein. While protein content should be somewhat limited, because it takes longer to digest and absorb than carbohydrates, protein intake will assist in avoiding sensations of hunger. Some examples of proteins include tuna, peanut butter, eggs, fish, chicken, and red meat. Also, limit the intake of fat, such as mayonnaise, butter, oil, salad dressing, sour cream, gravy, and margarine, because of the prolonged process of digestion, which could last up to eight hours. The problem with prolonged digestion during play is that some blood and energy stores that could be used by the exercising muscles will be redistributed to the stomach to aid in digestion.

Certain foods should be avoided, including foods with spicy ingredients that could cause heartburn and indigestion, and milk products, which can cause gastric distress in some players. Greasy foods should also be avoided because of the excess fat and the slower rates of digestion and emptying. The reference section at the back of the book includes websites to visit for more information on sound nutritional practices.

# Hydration—Drinking to Win

Research has indicated that water losses, through sweating, of 1 or 2 percent of body weight can impair mental and physical functioning (Chichester, 2002). When water is not replaced, total blood volume and oxygen delivery via the blood is impaired. The earliest symptoms of dehydration include loss of concentration and increased fatigue, since the brain and heart need water to maintain electrolyte balance and proper functioning. The more dehydrated athletes get, the more performance suffers. It has been reported by *Hydrate* (2002) that a 3 to 5 percent drop in fluid level causes a 10 percent drop in contractile strength, an 8 percent drop in speed, and can create headaches, dizziness, cramping, and nausea.

Athletes must not rely on thirst as an indicator of the need for water. Those who wait until this point can only put back between 50 and 75 percent of the body's need for fluids. In addition, knowing each player's weight pre- and postworkout can be a useful method of keeping track of weight loss. For each pound of weight lost, the player has lost one pint of fluid, and thus, needs to replace one pint of fluid. Over the course of a week, if players are losing five to 10 pounds, substantial fluid loss has taken place, since fat loss does not occur this quickly (Reimers & Ruud, 2002).

Each player should drink at least two cupfuls of water two hours before training or game play—allowing the kidneys 60 to 90 minutes to process excess fluids—and drink an additional one to two cups 15 minutes prior, which lowers the body's core temperature and replaces sweat loss. Additionally, sipping more water every 15 to 20 minutes during a game or practice should keep players properly hydrated. The more strenuous the training, the hotter the temperature, and the larger the athlete, the greater the fluid intake should be before, during, and after training or game play. Fluid loss also indicates a loss in electrolytes and sodium, both of which help regulate water distribution. Sport drinks are quite useful in replacing sodium, as well as critical electrolytes, including potassium, chloride, and magnesium.

Although some research has indicated that using urine color to regulate hydration levels is an inaccurate method, not all researchers agree. The old adage is to strive for a pale color after training or play. Players should be instructed to drink several cups of water and sport drinks postgame. Water is an ideal fluid replacement, though flavored sports drinks may promote greater drinking frequency, and these drinks may be more effective than water in rehydration, as they contain electrolytes, sugar, and carbohydrates. Sport drinks are especially effective if significant weight loss has occurred through sweating (Reimers & Ruud, 2002).

Courtesy of USC Sports Information

Figure 8-4. Making recovery training an active part of the practice routine helps players replenish their energy for game-time.

# Recovery—Eating and Drinking to Replenish

Research has shown that consuming carbohydrates and protein within 30 to 60 minutes after playing helps to reload muscles in 12 to 16 hours. If this window of opportunity is not taken advantage of, players may have less energy, which may affect motivation and drive the next day. The ratio of carbohydrates to proteins has been recommended to be three to one. For recovery purposes, carbohydrates restores muscle glycogen, while protein helps to repair and rebuild muscles and assists in transporting carbohydrates to the muscles (Liddane, 2002). Ed Burke, an expert in recovery and originator of the Endurox R4® sports drink, recommends that players eat a high-carbohydrate, high-protein snack within the recovery window. He also recommended that meals be eaten two to four hours postgame with the following nutritional make-up: carbohydrate (65 percent), fat (20 percent), and protein (15 percent) (Roberts, 2001).

# Chapter Summary

- It is very important for coaches to be careful in how they program intensity or stress levels to their players. Too little stress will result in underperforming and underachieving, while too much stress could result in training stress syndromes such as distress, staleness, or burnout.
- Consequences of coming into training camp undertrained could include negative effects on physiology, mental and emotional functioning, and skill training and performance.
- Distress and staleness are primarily caused by the physical and mental demands of increased training. Once stale, players who are exposed to greater increments of stress can begin exhibiting symptoms of burnout.
- For peak athletic performance, the two primary dietary goals for most elite athletes are eating to maximize performance and eating for optimal body composition.
- Research has shown that consuming carbohydrates and protein within 30 to 60 minutes after playing helps to reload muscles in 12 to 16 hours.

# 9

# Training for Automaticity II: Combating Technical-Tactical Barriers

## Technical/Tactical Proficiency

Improving upon players' technical mechanics, as well as improving the transfer of tactical lessons learned in practice onto the game field, requires deliberate effort on the part of both athletes and coaches. Because of its importance to optimal performance, improving upon deliberate practice is covered in full in Chapter 13, where a model is presented on improving upon the quality of practice by enhancing player and coach attitude, preparation, execution, and monitoring processes. Each component of the model includes numerous strategies that coaches and players can incorporate to improve technical and tactical execution.

Some athletes sabotage their technical and tactical execution prior to playing via mental misses. Mental misses can happen to any player. Consistent players usually have high levels of confidence and truly believe that something good will happen on any given possession. Consistent performers are usually very proficient at blocking out distractions and focusing on each play. They also relentlessly practice their craft. On the other hand, positional players who are "streaky" and inconsistent may not be physically and mentally committed to improving their total games. This lack of overall commitment can take many forms, including the belief that practicing fundamental techniques is a waste of time, that plays will be made in critical situations without practicing, and that going through the motions in practice instead of performing quality, focused repetitions is acceptable. Essentially, these players do not realize the importance of the mental side of passing, one-on-one attacking and defending, and shooting.

Inconsistent athletes could be missing key plays before the ball is played to them simply because they make too many mental mistakes prior to receiving the ball. Mental mistakes primarily occur across five mental-skill attributes:

- Confidence in abilities
- Trust in preparation and skills
- Focus on the important components of the skill, such as specific cues
- Commitment to improving skill execution in practice
- Executing one play at a time

Players who are fortunate enough to have these mental traits execute their skills in a smooth, effortless, automatic fashion. Players who "mentally miss" their chances normally lack one or more of these mental traits, or are unable to get back to their usual game when they are "off" and playing poorly. The next section describes seven different types of players, defined by their particular mental mistake.

# Typical Mental Misses

### The "Hit and Hope" Player

Once the ball leaves the foot, a "hit and hope" player prays that it gets to its primary target. This type of player lacks confidence in his ability to connect certain passes or make effective attacking passes, crossed balls, or shots on target. He lacks trust in his preparation, possibly because he has not prepared adequately enough through focused practice. He hopes that luck will be with these passes, crosses, and shots, almost relying on the "soccer gods" to deliver. Changing a "hit and hope" player into a consistent "playmaker" requires old-fashioned hard work and focused repetition, along with the realization that only he can change his practice habits and improve his confidence. Missed chances on goal, bad passes, and miscues are often the result of this type of thinking. Goalkeepers display these patterns when they flail away at crossed balls. Through game simulation, these goalkeepers should be prepared to go after crossed balls all over the box with or without traffic.

### The "Do or Die" Player

A player whose sole focus is on outcome, like being the game MVP or simply winning the game, can often distract himself enough to miss the play before it is happens. When a couple of plays do not go as planned, such errant passes or missed tackles, he is devastated. Although most of the pressure that players perceive is self-imposed, a few situations (e.g., taking a penalty kick) create actual pressure. A "do or die" player recognizes this pressure and heaps even more on himself by saying, "I need to make this shot…to keep the score close, to win the game, etc." or "If I miss another pass or tackle my coaches will be so upset." This increased pressure creates more stress that can get translated by the player into excess muscle tension or defeatist thinking, which are not advantageous to any player who is in need of fluid, relaxed execution. The section on the "flexed" player that follows discusses this issue in more detail. "Do or die" players need to learn how to focus more on the process of executing the skill and less on the outcome by using technical cues, which consist of one to two aspects of the needed skill. Midfielders may want to focus on a "good vision" or "smooth touch," or some other cue that helps the process of completing passes, rather than focusing only on how important a particular play may be.

## The "Fader" Player

A player who tends to "fade" in critical times is easily distracted by either internal or external distractions, or both. His focus fades from *external* distractions, such as the importance of the situation, crowd noise, or visual distractions, to *internal* distractions, such as how he is dealing with the pressure of the moment, the importance of the play, or on how he played the last time against this opponent. Since attentional capacity is limited, a player who attends to too many cues, especially irrelevant cues, sets himself up for mental misses, which have technical consequences, such as poorly timed saves and clearances for goalkeepers, or errant passes and missed goals—all due to "being too much in the head." This process is called "jamming," and is discussed in Chapter 7. Jamming occurs when athletes fail to focus on the most pertinent cues and information necessary for successful execution. A player who "fades" needs to work on being aware of what he is focusing on prior to, and during, play execution. Once he is aware of where his focus lies, the next step is to focus only on the most relevant cues. Coaches can be a big help in assisting players in this process. Once players consistently focus on specific cues, the distractions will be blocked out, resulting with an automated, free-flowing performance.

## The "Flexed" Player

A player who is "flexed" is tight and tense due to his fear of missing plays, such as tackles, passes, headers, or shots. Fear of making mistakes and failing can trigger the "flight or fight" response, which prepares the body for a threat. In doing so, the body reacts with increased heart rate, muscle tension, and a clutter of distracting thoughts. This excessive tension could be felt especially in the chest, shoulders, and legs, causing shortness of breath and turning a normally smooth action into rigid, stiff motion. This stiffer motion disrupts fluid, rhythmic technical and physical form. A change in technical form, often called pressing, can be reversed by learning how to relax these critical muscle groups via muscle-relaxation exercises, relaxation breathing, and mistake-management routines that can enhance mental and physical readiness. However, a player who is aware of "pressing" is well on his way to changing his performance woes. Chapter 12 describes the use of routines to enhance technical execution in greater detail.

## The "Hot and Cold" Player

A "hot and cold" player is simply streaky. When "hot footed," he will complete his passes and make plays. But if any part of his game is off, he carries it with him to the next possession or one-on-one dual, resulting in "cold" spells. Truly competitive players are able to remain consistent in their play by being consistent "thinkers." They do not allow swings in game momentum or periods of good/poor play to cause them to change their approach, confidence, and readiness. A consistently high level of playing confidence can be ensured through pregame routines, coping routines (used to help refocus after mistakes or great plays by opponents), positive imagery, and self-coaching affirmations. These techniques are discussed in detail in Chapter 12.

## The "Mechanical" Player

A "mechanical" player allows his left brain to dominate his processing by focusing too much of his attention on the specific mechanics of the necessary technique. These technical motions should be so habitual and well-learned that thinking about particular elements right before execution causes major distractions, such as focusing on getting over the ball to keep the shot low. Having sound mental mechanics means being able to stay focused on productive elements prior to execution, thus freeing the mind of distraction. Doing so results in automatic execution—a point worth repeating.

Establishing a consistent coping routine is critical for mechanical players, because these players, especially, struggle with letting go of mistakes and moving on to the next possession and attacking/defending opportunity. Keeping in mind one to two general cues is recommended, such as "smooth" or "head on a swivel" for midfielders and attackers. These general cues are linked to specific actions, which helps to ensure efficient mechanics. "Smooth," for example, is recited prior to the reception, because the player has programmed this word to mean a relaxed, smooth, automatic reception. The use of multiple technical cues is not recommended, because it internally distracts the "mechanical" player and causes him to think too much prior to delivery. All players can benefit from the use of general cues, which help to free their minds and automatically execute when called upon.

## The "Counter" Player

A player who gets caught up counting his missed tackles, poor first touches, missed chances to score, botched saves and crossed balls, and playing time—especially from game to game—is only bringing (or keeping) himself down via lowered confidence and heightened anxiety. Meanwhile, he is heightening the pressure for successful future outcomes. Players who know exactly how many mistakes they have made are too outcome-focused and are guilty of being "counters." To break the cycle of counting these miscues, players must begin to become process- rather than outcome-focused by taking one play at a time and utilizing a consistent routine for coping with and moving past mistakes. Counting mistakes will only lead to more missed plays.

Courtesy of Duke University Sports Information

Figure 9-1. Top competitors are able to combat mental misses.

## Chapter Summary

- Inconsistent players could be missing key plays before the ball is sent in their direction because they make too many mental mistakes prior to the play.
- Mental mistakes occur across five mental-skill attributes: confidence, trust, focus, commitment, and the execution of one play at a time.
- Mental mistakes encompass being short of confidence ("hit and hope" players), too outcome-focused ("do or die" players), too easily distracted ("fader" players), too tight and tense ("flexed" players), too streaky ("hot and cold" players), too analytical ("mechanical" players), and prone to counting mistakes ("counter" players).
- Players who mentally miss their chances can combat their barriers by enhancing their mental toughness skills.

# 10

# Training for Automaticity III: Combating Team Barriers

Effective teamwork can often be the difference between success and failure, as exemplified by the paradox whereby teams full of talented players fail to use their individual resources and fall short of expectations, while teams with less talent and resources prevail (Hardy & Crace, 1997). Effective teamwork can be seen in teams that do the following (Carron, Spink, & Prapavessis, 1997; Yukelson, 1997):

- Take advantage of the various abilities and backgrounds of team members.
- Interact and work toward shared goals.
- Balance the needs of the team with the needs of the individual members.
- Structure methods of communication.

The many barriers that can sabotage a team's pursuit of greatness are covered in Chapter 6. These barriers include an unwillingness to sacrifice for the team, poor communication, lack of quality practice, inability to hold teammates accountable, unwillingness to help teammates, and lack of trust. Lencioni (2002) identified additional team barriers in a book titled *The 5 Dysfunctions of a Team*, which include absence of trust, fear of conflict, lack of commitment, avoidance of accountability, and inattention to results. According to Lencioni, an absence of trust means that team members are not open with each other about their thoughts and feelings. In such a situation, team members are not honest about their feedback for fear of conflict and of having to share real ideas in an open discussion. Due to an inability to openly share ideas, team members do not commit to team decision and objectives. Since team members do not share common ideals, an avoidance of accountability exists, which then leads to an overindulgence of individual agendas, rather than a collective effort toward team objectives.

Successfully defeating these barriers will create teams consisting of members who trust one another enough to have open discussions, which will lead to a greater commitment to team ideals. This commitment will allow team members to hold each other accountable to these standards, thus leading to a collective effort toward achieving team goals. Team trust is a fragile concept, because if one element is lacking, fallout will occur. This chapter emphasizes several examples that coaches and teams can utilize to steer clear from these barriers and prosper, collectively.

An intervention called team-building, which is designed to positively affect group processes and performance, can be utilized to assist coaches and players in enhancing upon these critical components of effective teamwork, while also steering clear of team barriers. The aim of these team-building strategies is to get all team members "on the same page" in terms of the team's direction and primary objectives, as well as forge an agreement on the execution standards and everyone's particular roles and responsibilities. A carefully designed team-building program is a proactive way to combat potential team barriers before they occur. Although using a program does not guarantee total team harmony, it provides coaches and players with a forum to discuss goals, team rules, and standards, and address potential problem areas before they develop. The framework behind this sample team-building program consists of the following components:

- Team motives and preferences for team progress
- An accepted team identity—what the team will be known for by others
- A shared vision via setting short-term, process goals that lead to accomplishing long-term, outcome goals
- Individual and team accountability to preset standards and goals
- Collaborative communication, teamwork, and trust
- Team-bonding activities in the off-season, preseason, and during the season

# Individual/Team Motives

One way to maximize a player's motivation is to match his preferences and motives with your own motives and behaviors. For example, a player whose primary motive is to improve upon his game enough to earn a scholarship at a top school is going to want demanding technical sessions, and thus would prefer a coach who will encourage him to accomplish this goal. If the player's preferences and motives are matched, he will be more satisfied and motivated to pursue his goals. On the other hand, if the player's preferences and motives are not matched by the coach, dissatisfaction and underachievement may result. This dynamic also applies to team motives and preferences.

> *"When the team's goals are consistent with a player's professional goals, that player is a lot more likely to be a team player."*
> —Pat Williams, Senior Executive Vice President, Orlando Magic,
> *The Magic of Teamwork* (p. 129)

Gaining a better understanding of player and team motives and preferences can aid in not only maximizing motivation, but also in getting everyone "on the same page" regarding the goals for the team. Obtaining this information is as easy as asking each player what his primary motives are for playing, and what teammate and coach behaviors he prefers. To get a better idea of what specific preferences your players have in terms of the feedback provided to them by coaches and teammates, ask them to do the following:

- List three things you would like to see the *coaches* do/say this pre-season/season that would help:
  ✓ This team accomplish its goals

  ✓ You accomplish your goals

- List three things you would like to see your *teammates* do/say this pre-season/ season that would help:
  ✓ This team accomplish its goals

  ✓ You accomplish your goals

This information will give coaches a better idea of what "buttons" to push with each of the players. You certainly do not have to always abide by these preferences, but they do provide a guideline. For example, if a player says that he would like to see his coaches "get on me when I lose focus or when I begin to go through the motions," the coaches have gained some valuable information in terms of the best method by which to get this player back into the game mentally.

# Team Identity

Getting an idea of how the team would like to be perceived by others, such as opponents, fans, or family, is another way of getting the most from your players. Asking the team to clarify their "team identity" can elicit player feedback regarding goals, motives, and how they would like to be seen and known by others. Armed with this information, coaches can hold their team accountable to this ideal team image. Ask each member the following questions:

- How would you want opponents to view the team?
- How would you like to be perceived during practices; what would spectators of the practices say about the team?
- How would you want your team to be perceived by game officials or the media?

Use this information to help develop your team identity. Once an identity is established, any time you see that players are not showing their chosen identity, remind them about it. Also emphasize when you do see them demonstrating the ideal they have created. More will be said about these "coachable moments" later in this chapter.

---

*"This game ... can give you a lot of things, but it can't give you a championship. You've got to earn that. And unless you're willing to pay the collective price—to play as a team—you will not get it."*
—Bill Parcells, Former Head Coach, Dallas Cowboys
(Williams, 1997, p. 115)

---

# Team and Individual Goals

Setting goals is effective in influencing performance by enhancing motivation, self-confidence, commitment, effort, and mental readiness. Research has shown that pursuing goals conveys information to the players about their capabilities and progress, thus enhancing confidence and motivation to continue striving toward excellence. A common analogy used to describe the goal-setting process states that setting effective goals is similar to using a road map before embarking on a long trip. Mapping the way before a trip is obviously important for arriving at the destination safely and efficiently. Applying this thinking to a team's journey to a predetermined destination, whether that is a conference, state, or national championship, is highly recommended.

To kick-start this goal-setting process, present the following questions to your players:
- What would you like to be doing with soccer in five years?
- What do you want to accomplish in soccer this year?
- What does this team want to accomplish this year?
- What are some areas of your game that you need to improve?
- What are some areas that the team needs to improve?

Having players complete these questions, especially during the off-season or preseason practice, will get them thinking about their own games as well as the team game, and what must be improved upon. Players' responses to these questions can then be shared with the coach and used to devise short- and long-term goals. Individual and team goals can be quite empowering if used properly through shared input and continual evaluation and follow-up.

SMART goals are recommended to develop a goal-setting program for your players and team:

S = Specific: Do not set "do-your-best" goals, but instead identify specific aspects needing improvement (also called action goals).

M = Measurable: You should be able to evaluate whether a goal was achieved via the use of numbers or objective measures.

A = Achievable: A goal should be within a player's or team's capabilities.

R = Realistic: All goals should be challenging—not too easy and not too difficult.

T = Time-based: You should be able to assign a set target date when a goal will be achieved.

Each of the various types of goals has its proper place in the goal-setting process. Outcome goals, though many players may find them motivating, should be used minimally, since outcomes may be beyond a player's immediate control. Examples of outcome goals include winning games, championships, and awards.

Process goals should be used as steppingstones (short-term goals) that lead players to accomplish their long-range goals. These short-term, process goals should be specific technical, tactical, mental, and/or physical aspects that players are driven to accomplish. When players attend to process goals, outcomes will tend to take care of themselves. Goal-achievement strategies include how players plan to accomplish the short-term goals and improve upon their weaker areas in practice and games (specific drills, actions, thoughts).

Another important aspect of setting goals is feedback, which is when SMART goals become so critical. SMART goals, by nature, provide internal feedback to the player. Was the goal accomplished? If not, what went wrong? External feedback from coaches is also critical to the goal-setting process. Players should set their own goals, but obtaining suggestions in terms of specific areas in need of attention is very important. Continual feedback from coaches in terms of goal progress (or goal revision) is also critical.

Courtesy of John Voight

Figure 10-1. Setting SMART goals can help guide a team toward success.

The following examples highlight the use of SMART goals for strikers and midfielders:

- This week in practice I will improve my passing efficiency by completing seven of 10 passes in our possession play.
- I am going to improve my field vision by watching extra game/practice video for 20 minutes before/after each practice so that I can see what I've been missing (open players, flank and overlapping runs, passing seams).
- This week in practice I will improve my ability to let go of errors by practicing my coping routine during the scrimmage.
- By next Friday, I will learn all of the new set plays by having the coach test me for several minutes before and during each practice this week.

Players can learn from goals being accomplished ("keep doing what I've been doing") and from those goals that are not being met ("since what I'm doing is not working, what changes must be made?"). At this point, coaches can offer instruction on what needs to be changed. Having players and coaches monitor progress on predetermined goals will be valuable on a consistent basis. The more that coaches refer to these goals and reinforce any progress made toward accomplishing them, the more empowering they will become for the players.

One way to present individual or team goals to your players or team is to insert these goals onto a staircase diagram. The idea is for them to see that before they can proceed to the next stair, or goal, the previous goal needs to be accomplished. The goals nearer the bottom of the staircase can be preseason goals, followed by the in-season goals, topped with some postseason goals. Figure 10-2 is an example of a goal staircase that follows these progressions for the entire team. These goals include short- and long-range goals and process and outcome goals. This goal staircase can either be given to each player or be posted in the team room, locker room, or out on the practice field. Moreover, these goal staircases can be specific to each position, since each positional unit will have their own standards and goals.

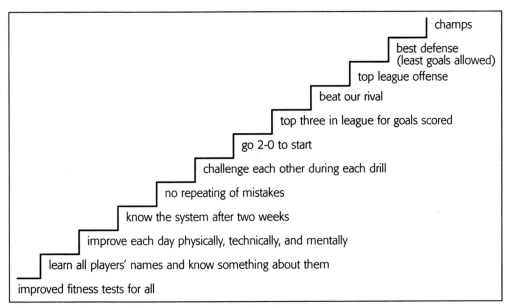

Figure 10-2. Short- and long-range team goal staircase

# Accountability

Continually referring back to goals, definitions, the team identity, and practice standards is critical to achieving lasting effects. Holding players accountable to these goals and standards is a little easier because the players helped to devise them. One of the better ways of keeping the players accountable to these standards is to have them rate their progress and evaluate what areas need continual improvement. By providing continual evaluation and encouragement, as well as allowing players the opportunity to voice their opinions on important team issues, coaches can increase their sense of responsibility, ownership, and commitment to the team's efforts. Have players rate their progress on each of the goals and standards on a scale of 1 to 10 (1 equals "no progress" and 10 equals a "total change for the better"). Obtaining an team average for each goal and standard can lead to an active discussion about what the team has done well (or not done well) to accomplish the changes, as well as what needs to happen to continue the progress and improvement.

Courtesy of Dartmouth Sports Information

Figure 10-3. It is crucial for coaches to offer feedback regarding goal progress and take full advantage of coachable moments to help reinforce team standards.

The key component of a goal-setting program is getting players to govern and police themselves with regards to team rules, standards, and communication procedures. Once this environment exists, a team becomes "player driven" as opposed to "coach driven." Marty Schottenheimer, former head coach of the San Diego Chargers, echoes this sentiment: "The most successful teams that I've been around were those where the players drove the machine" (Didenger, 1995).

Meeting regularly with players individually and with the team as a whole, coupled with an open line of communication, allows players to voice their opinions in an open forum and gives each team member a say in the workings of the team. Keep in mind that players should be allowed to provide feedback and dialogue on team issues only (e.g., standards, goals, rules), not on playing time/status issues, scheduling, practice activities, or game strategy, which is reserved for the coaching staff. Former NFL coach

Dennis Green offers some good advice by warning coaches about taking this feedback too far: "A common mistake made by some coaches is they let their superstars write their own rules" (*Los Angeles Times*, 2003c).

When teams or positional units are not able to challenge themselves to maintain the standards set by the team, then the coaches need to step in and dish out some sort of predetermined punishment. If the captains are not leading the way as needed, then new captains may need to be chosen. Starters who are not modeling the correct behaviors must become nonstarters for a spell. Dishing out punishment must be calculated and not done with haste; it takes time to find the right "buttons" to push to lead to behavior change. Making players perform extra conditioning may make the coaches feel better, but does it allow the team to grow closer as a unit? This punishment may work for some teams, but taking away responsibility and playing time usually speaks louder than a coach's whistle. Taking advantage of those "coachable moments" can really assist in developing into a team mindset. Coachable moments include times when players make sacrifices for the greater good, like hustling for another teammate, finishing off sprints to set good examples, not allowing other players to complain about a drill, or challenging teammates to give quality repetitions. So many coaches are too quick to point out when things are not working that they fail to take advantage of those moments when teams are clicking and playing as one.

> *"Being the best is a simple decision... It's not glamorous. It's not about glory or God-given talent. It's about commitment, plain and simple. But saying you want to be at the very top of your field and doing it are two different things. The bottom line is, if I don't go into it every day consistently committed, I won't get results."*
> —Mia Hamm, Olympic/World Cup Champion Soccer Star
> (Dorfman, 2003, p. 258)

A final note about accountability is the importance of player commitment to the goals and standards of the team. Players who have a high level of commitment have already "bought what the team is selling" and will do what needs to be done for the team to be successful. Jeff Janssen (2002) lists six different levels of commitment in his book entitled *Championship Team Building*. These levels can be described as existing on a continuum, from the least committed, called the resistant phase, to the higher degrees of commitment, called committed and compelled. After reading through the definitions of each type of player, ask yourself how many of your players fall into each category. The commitment continuum consists of the following:

- Resistant players are on a different page than the rest of the team and are motivated by their own agenda.
- Reluctant players do enough to get by, but are not truly on board.

- Existent players are driven by other motives that do not match those of the overall team, so the commitment level to the team goals suffers.
- Compliant players are those who do what is asked of them and understand the importance of collective action.
- Committed players are those who are not only compliant, but put in extra energy to help the team succeed.
- Compelled players are totally driven by the team's pursuit and do all they can to assist.

According to Janssen (2002), championship teams consist primarily of players in the "compliant" to "compelled" categories. Where are the majority of your players? Posting this commitment continuum on a board for the team to see and use to self-assess where they perceive themselves to be can be interesting. Coaches can then compare where they thought each player was on the commitment continuum and where the player perceived himself to be. This chapter provides strategies for improving player commitment to the team pursuit.

---

*"When a team outgrows individual performance and learns team confidence, excellence becomes a reality."*

—Joe Paterno, Head Football Coach, Penn State
(Williams, 1997, p. 8)

---

# Team Communication

Effective team communication and teamwork are often taken for granted. What works with one team does not necessarily work for another. Breakdowns in communication—coach to player, player to player, or player to coach—are often the cause of conflict. Ensuring that all parties are practicing effective communication techniques is essential for optimal teamwork and achievement on the soccer field.

Team meetings should be conducted to learn more about communication issues, the consequences of ineffective communication, and ways to improve. Major topics to discuss include the importance of sending effective messages, as well as of receiving messages effectively (Figure 10-4).

---

*"If you cannot relate (establish a relationship) to today's player, you're through as a coach."*

—Steve Mariucci, Former Head Coach, Detroit Lions
(Dorfman, 2003, p. 42)

---

*Sending Effective Verbal Messages*

- Be direct and specific
- Be clear and consistent
- Focus on one thing at a time
- Be consistent with what is being said and subsequent nonverbal messages
- Deliver messages immediately

*Receiving Effective Verbal Messages*

- Be an active listener (paying attention, giving appropriate feedback, and good nonverbal communication, e.g., eye contact)
- Be a supportive listener (value the speaker and the message)

Figure 10-4. Sending and receiving messages

It is important for players and coaches to be aware of the "external signs" that they are emitting during practice or matches. These external signs consist of nonverbal cues, body language, posture, gestures, and facial expressions (e.g., rolling the eyes, looking away) that may be perceived as positive, negative, or neutral. Those behaviors perceived as neutral or negative are not conducive to open communication. Many players hurt themselves by not being aware of their nonverbal behaviors, especially in stressful times. A player can cast himself in a negative light if he shows too many negative nonverbal behaviors. The same can happen to coaches.

As Figure 10-4 shows, breakdowns in communication can occur due to faulty messages (either sending or receiving) via both verbal and nonverbal communication methods. Coaches who are cognizant of the verbal and nonverbal communication patterns of their team (player to player, player to coach, coach to player) will be in a better position to step in if the need arises and intervene appropriately. The most common consequences of ineffective communication are frustration, anger, dissatisfaction, withdrawal, derision between teammates, frequent confrontations, and the formation of cliques (i.e., teammates begin to take sides). These situations can be avoided if the team discusses the importance of effective communication practices and identifies how to improve upon team communication.

Communication standards set by coaches and their players should be evaluated often in terms of team progress. With any team, conflicts can occur throughout the season, but since time has been taken to set up communication standards, it will be easier to define the problems and suggest ways of correcting them. Teams that follow the "10 Commandments" of communication (Anshel, 1990) help establish an excellent standard of open communication for their players and coaches. This list in

Figure 10-5 has been modified to specifically address team communication practices for coaches and players.

Being honest and consistent means telling players what they need to hear rather than what they want to hear. The fight against mediocrity is a taxing, constant battle that requires coaches to encourage, confront, and challenge players on a daily basis. The same goes for players who truly want to challenge each other to get better. This skill may need to be taught to some players or teams.

This statement may sound a bit simplistic, but being a good listener means improving upon the skill of active listening. Allowing someone the opportunity to voice his opinions is hard for most people, especially listening without judging and getting defensive. Being open to new and different ideas is a critical component of being an active listener. Doing so also means breaking out of comfort zones. Every team player must feel comfortable about speaking to the coach and teammates if he has problems or issues to share. Players who are too quiet and shy do not get their opinions voiced, and therefore usually do whatever everyone else does. These players may be quite dissatisfied with an issue that will go unresolved due to their unwillingness to bring it up. Coaches are primarily responsible for creating a climate in which players have the ability to offer their insights without hesitation.

Another important aspect of improving team communication, particularly among the players, is empathy, or putting yourself in someone else's shoes via "trying on" their thoughts and feelings. Coaches who can also acknowledge the many variables impacting players' performance and well-being will be better prepared to help if needed.

Thou shalt
…be honest and consistent
…be a good listener
…break out of comfort zones
…be empathetic
…never be sarcastic
…be specific and productive with feedback
…trust teammates and coaches
…be able to productively challenge teammates
…not allow teammates to drift
…use productive nonverbal behaviors

Figure 10-5. The "10 Commandments" of effective team communication

Figure 10-6. USC players wear their team standards on the back of their training shirts, which serves to remind them of what must be done daily.

Sarcastic feedback to players and teammates serves one purpose—to beat down the player on the receiving end. Confidence gets hit hard by mindless sarcasm. Being critical is one thing; being sarcastic is another. Sarcasm should not be a part of anyone's arsenal of methods used to improve motivation, as it usually accomplishes exactly the opposite.

Coaches use two forms of constructive feedback: positive and productive feedback. Positive feedback ("you are a really good player") helps players feel better about themselves. This feeling may lead to increased confidence and improved performance. But competitive athletes want more than the "warm fuzzies." They want specific performance cues or teaching points, called productive feedback, regarding what worked and what did not work (and why). Being positive only gets players so far. Offering productive feedback gives detailed comments to athletes about their performance, rather than simply stroking their egos. Enough people are around who will "pump up" players' egos (family, friends), and more is usually not needed.

Trusting teammates and coaches means not having to question their beliefs, drive, commitment, work ethic, desire, expertise, and talent. A lot of the friction that occurs within a team stems from a lack of trust. Players who doubt the decisions made by the coaching staff (treatment of players, playing time, play calling), and coaches who believe that players are putting themselves before the team, are two common situations that illustrate a lack of team trust. Once trust is established, teammates can then begin to productively challenge their teammates. In most cases, this challenge means telling a teammate that he needs to give more to the team, such as more effort and a greater commitment. Yet once practice or games are over, friendships should still be intact. The ability to challenge teammates is more a matter of trust than it is about being assertive.

*"I truly believe that when you're trying to find out who your true guys are, there are probably 20% that are winners, 20% that are losers, and 60% looking for direction. So you put the onus on them... It's accountability, responsibility, and trust. You trust that the guy next to you is doing his job, that he's doing his homework, that he's working the trade."*
—George O'Leary, Former NFL Coach; Current Head Coach, University of Central Florida (*USA Today*, 2003, p. 2C)

If teams truly want to excel, helping each other push beyond individual comfort zones is a prerequisite. Caution must be given to the tone and delivery of this feedback, however. Being productive means providing useful information and a rationale for the feedback, not simply yelling at teammates (negative feedback). Also,

Figure 10-7. The content, delivery, and timing of feedback can be critical to team effectiveness.

> *"When a team is united, it won't make any difference what outsiders think… Your competition will have fewer weaknesses to exploit. But a team divided against itself can break down at any moment. The least bit of pressure or adversity will crack it apart."*
> —Bill Parcells, Former Head Coach, Dallas Cowboys
> (Williams, 1997, p. 147)

be mindful of the use of productive nonverbal behaviors, because a lot can be told from how players carry themselves, especially in tough times. Finally, players cannot allow a teammate to drift or separate from the team due to his frustrations with his own play (especially mistakes). Instead, they should help to bring him back into the mix through positive, productive encouragement, high fives, pats on the back, or even specific technical advice.

# Team-Bonding Activities

For years, coaches from all types of team sports have incorporated team-bonding activities to complement their training sessions before the start of the season. One of the primary goals for these team-bonding activities is to help teammates get to know each other and begin to form bonds, so when the pressure of the season begins, these bonds are tight enough for the team to persevere and thrive. This process is referred to as team cohesion and consists of two interactive components: task cohesion and social cohesion. Task cohesion reflects the ability of the team to work together toward common goals, while social cohesion refers to the closeness between teammates (Carron, Spink, & Prapavessis, 1997).

The ideal situation is for teams to be strong in both task and social cohesion. A team that likes hanging together off the field, as well as working hard together on the field, is in a better position to be successful. Teams that suffer from cliques, personality clashes, poor communication practices, and daily confrontations will struggle with social cohesion. Poor social cohesion can obviously have a negative impact on how willing these players are to put in maximal, collective efforts on the field. Team-building intervention programs can help coaches and teams improve upon both components of cohesion. Specifically, taking players through goal-setting, standard-setting, and other brainstorming sessions can them get on the "same page" and improve task cohesion, while team-bonding activities have been found to be effective in improving team social cohesion.

A *Sports Illustrated* article (McCallum, 2001) detailed how many top collegiate football programs incorporate team-building activities into their summer "voluntary" conditioning sessions, with some even adopting the credo "bond in the heat and we

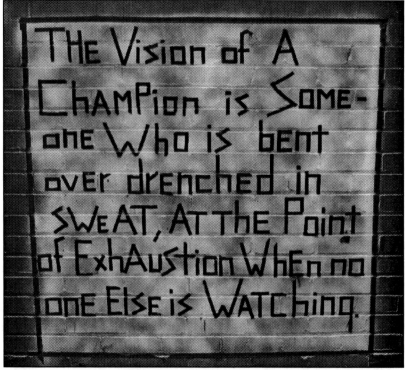

Courtesy of Rudie Voight

Figure 10-8. Having teams participate in team-bonding activities, such painting motivational messages in the locker room or out on the practice field, can go a long way to building social and task cohesion.

can't be beat!" For example, University of Oregon players rafted down the Willamette River, while the Mississippi Bulldogs endured Army-like basic-training exercises. Other anecdotes included players from Louisiana State University taking part in karate training, and the Fighting Illini playing in a football-player-only Wednesday night softball league. The Hokies from Virginia Tech hit several stops along the NASCAR circuit, while players from Texas Tech engaged in organized sparring sessions with local boxers. Although varied, these team-building activities were all organized to create a more closely knit team that would then (hopefully) win games in September. Some teams may go to a comedy club or have a team bowling tournament, movie night, pot-luck dinner, scavenger hunt, white-water rafting trip, outdoor adventure course, or camping trip. Coaches are limited only by their imagination.

*"The trust we'll have in one another during the season will have been built in the summer, and there's no way you can overvalue trust on a football team."*

—Ryan Schmid, Center, University of Oregon
(McCallum, 2001, p. 76)

# Team-Building Implementation

Applying the six components described previously entails packaging them into a team-building intervention program. The following stages incorporate general implementation procedures and specific application strategies to a team-building intervention program that can be used for soccer teams.

## Stage 1

A formal needs assessment is conducted by coaches who specifically attempt to answer the following question: What does this team need to do to be successful? Coaches should think in terms of the physical, technical, strategic, team, mental, emotional, and inspirational capacities, which were discussed in Chapter 3.

## Stage 2

Using this information, coaches develop a specific plan that addresses how they can get the team to improve upon these needs. Decisions regarding the exact team-bonding activities and team-building meeting topics should be made at this time as well.

## Stage 3

An initial team meeting should be conducted between the team and coaches that consists of an educational orientation about what team building is and presents guidelines for optimal team communication. The coach can then facilitate brainstorming sessions on what the team needs to do to be successful. Coaches can list their own comments on a blackboard, along with comments from the players. This meeting is the ideal time to have players think and record their primary motives for playing, as well as their specific preferences for coach and teammate behaviors and feedback.

## Stage 4

The team prioritizes the input (i.e., the most important needs), and then additional brainstorming is conducted to define each point and how it can be assessed and accounted for in action words. This step is important because defining each strategy puts a "face on it." Another meeting point could include establishing a team identity.

## Stage 5

Follow-up meetings can be conducted to develop short- and long-range goals, action plans that detail how these goals will be achieved, team rules, and standards of execution.

## Stage 6

Follow-up meetings can include an evaluation of team progress on their standards and goals (via rating sheets and open discussions), and progress on team cohesion and team communication. It is absolutely critical to provide feedback and evaluation to the players for the intervention to have maximal effect.

## Stage 7

Team meetings can then be set up to deal with conflicts that may occur during the season, as well as incorporate some team-cohesion activities in the midst of the season, such as team meals and outings to continue to foster task and social cohesion.

Courtesy of Dartmouth Sports Information

Figure 10-9. Coaching today's athletes means giving of yourself by showing your commitment to them as people and players.

# Chapter Summary

- Effective teamwork can often be the difference between success and failure.
- A carefully designed team-building program is a proactive way to combat potential team barriers before they occur.
- Asking the team to identify its "team identity" is another method of obtaining player feedback regarding goals, motives, and how they would like to be seen by others.
- Setting SMART goals is recommended.
- Players can learn from goals being accomplished, as well as from those that are not being met.
- Breakdowns in communication are often the cause of conflicts, from coach to player, player to player, or player to coach.
- The fight against mediocrity is a taxing, constant battle that requires coaches willing to encourage, confront, and challenge players on a daily basis.
- Team-building intervention programs include brainstorming team motives and preferences, team identity, goals, methods of accountability, collaborative communication and trust, and team-bonding activities, all of which are designed to improve social and task team cohesion.

# 11

# Applying Mental Toughness Training to Everyday Coaching

It is critical for coaches to realize that teaching mental toughness skills to their players is similar to presenting and teaching technical skills and play calls. Moreover, most coaches already present mental skills to their players and teams in their everyday coaching without even knowing it.

## Everyday Application of Mental-Skill Strategies

Many coaches appreciate the importance of the mental side of their sports and attempt to get this information across to their players. Others feel that mental-skills training is too time consuming, should only be used with athletes in slumps or with only the most elite athletes, or is just not effective. The major aim of this chapter is to demystify mental-skills training for skeptic coaches, while also educating all coaches about fundamental ways of incorporating mental-skills training into their everyday coaching.

The five mental-skill methods that have been found to be important for consistent, optimal performance are the use of imagery, goal setting, pre-performance routines, concentration training, and intensity regulation. After reading the following sections, ask yourself how many of these mental-skill methods you are presently using in your everyday coaching.

Courtesy of USC Sports Information

Figure 11-1. Successful coaches find many ways of teaching the mental side of the game to their players during practice and game-time feedback.

## Imagery

Use of imagery includes the following:
- Using video breakdowns and highlight tapes (McCann, 2001)
- Using scouting reports
- Performing walk-throughs of the competition site prior to playing
- Using creative language that helps to give players a clearer "picture" when learning complex sports skills (McCann, 2001), such as teaching players to put their "head on a swivel" to improve vision, so that they are always looking around prior to receiving the ball
- Performing walk-throughs of plays and strategies during practice
- Mentally rehearsing plays, routines, or technical drills before physically doing them
- Mentally picturing the pitch or large crowd the night before
- Modeling technical execution via seeing it, feeling it, and repeating it

All of these coaching strategies incorporate the use of imagery to aid in learning skills and tactics, preparation, and performance execution. If you use some or all of these methods, you have been teaching your players one of the key mental-skill methods. Chapter 12 offers more details and additional ways of incorporating imagery into your coaching.

## Goal Setting

Helping athletes and teams set goals is an effective exercise to enhance team building, team motivation, and process-oriented behavior. Goal setting includes the following:
- Giving players a verbal or written practice plan
- Giving players a verbal or written game plan
- Describing specific objectives for the week of practice, or at the beginning of each individual practice
- Targeting specific performance areas that the team needs to improve upon
- Conducting team meetings to discuss what is needed for the team to have a successful season
- Defining roles and responsibilities for each member of your team
- Continuously reminding players of areas in which they need to improve

Setting goals has been proven by research and reports from elite athletes to be effective in influencing performance by enhancing player motivation, self-confidence, commitment, effort, and mental readiness. Pursuing specific short-term goals on the way to achieving longer-term goals conveys reliable information to the athlete about their capabilities and progress. When an athlete is making progress toward a goal, confidence, commitment, and motivation increase.

## Pre-performance Routines

At the elite level, where athletes possess similar sport-specific and physical abilities, the way athletes engage their thoughts and emotions before a competition could be the difference between winning and losing. When players think about negative things and get down on themselves, they usually play their worst games, while those who think productively and find ways of keeping themselves feeling good end up having their better performances. One of the most important factors contributing to top performance is the ability to generate and maintain optimal readiness prior to competition. One method of improving physical, mental, and emotional readiness is the use of pre-performance routines. The following list details the many ways in which you may already be utilizing preparatory routines in your coaching:
- Establishing a schedule for pregame activities, such as meetings, meals, treatment, and dressing
- Establishing a schedule for prepractice activities
- Allowing players some "free" time before the game for personal preparation activities
- Walking through specific warm-up activities to ensure effective execution
- Using pregame pep talks to energize the squad
- Giving players individualized feedback prior to games to energize, relax, motivate, increase confidence, or instruct

All of these preparatory strategies incorporate many different components, including motivational components (pep talks, individual talks with players), technical aspects (pregame coaching points), and attempts to enhance confidence, cope with anxiety and concentration, and increase readiness. Several methods that players can utilize to develop their own pre-performance routines are presented later in this chapter.

## Concentration Training

Attentional focus is the ability to focus on the most relevant information during play. Attentional switching is the ability to adjust the attentional focus (width and direction) depending upon the particular sport situation. Concentration training includes the following:

- Instructing players on specific performance cues
- Offering coaching points to players that direct them toward specific technical or strategical elements of play during games and practices
- Calling time-outs to help players focus on important elements of the next play
- Using simulation training, such as piping in crowd noise or using your opponent's tactics/formations, during practice to prepare players for game-like conditions

Courtesy of Western Mass Pioneers

Figure 11-2. Coaches must learn as much as possible about each of their players to maximize their capacities for optimal, consistent play, which entails going beyond just the skills, drills, and X's and O's.

## Intensity Regulation

Gaining control over the level of intensity is one of the most important things athletes can do to improve upon their practice and game readiness (mental toughness). Levels of intensity are specific to each athlete. Some athletes perform better when they have low levels of intensity (very relaxed), while others need a moderate level (a composed intensity), and still others need a high level of intensity (pumped up!). Intensity regulation includes the following:

- Using pregame pep talks to "pump up" the squad
- Instructing players to stay composed rather than let their emotions take over. For example, tell players to not "lose control" when plays go against them or when they experience other adversities (e.g., a perceived injustice, such as lack of playing time).
- Attempting to predict which players are nervous and which are too relaxed based upon "outward signs" and body language. Some coaches believe that every player needs to be pumped up to be ready to play, so they look for these visible behaviors and actions.
- Telling players to "relax" when they appear uptight and nervous

Being able to relax is an important mental skill that some coaches just assume their players have. Realizing that each player differs in terms of his preference for intensity level, coaches must work with each player to figure out what level works best. This topic is covered in more detail in Chapter 13.

How many of these mental-skill strategies have you incorporated with your players and team? To those coaches who utilize a great number of these fundamental methods, congratulations! You have been implementing some critical mental-skill strategies for the betterment of your players and teams. Coaches who are not utilizing these strategies are missing out on some great opportunities to improve upon their players' preparation and execution skills. All coaches can challenge themselves further by implementing additional mental-skill methods, as described in Chapter 12. A quick tip on incorporating mental-skill training into everyday coaching is to assess each drill for how it can develop a particular mental skill or technique, much like coaches do to test physical, technical, and tactical applications. For example, during a six-versus-two possession drill, the coach can reinforce composure ("first touch away from oncoming defensive pressure"), communication with fellow attackers (or defenders), moving past mistakes, and anticipation (taking a look prior to the ball arriving to take advantage of environmental cues). Specific team components can be tested, such as how the team rallies through adversity (having to do a lot of sprints or a demanding drill) and who takes on the leadership roles. Many more tips can be found in Chapters 12 and 13.

# Chapter Summary

- Most coaches already incorporate mental skills into their everyday coaching without even knowing it.
- The five mental-skill methods that are important for consistent, optimal performance are the use of imagery, goal setting, pre-performance routines, concentration training, and intensity regulation.
- Coaches who are not utilizing many of the mental-skill strategies mentioned in this chapter are missing some great opportunities to improve upon their players' preparation and execution skills.

# 12

# Training for Automaticity IV: Combating Mental Barriers— Training for Tough Thinking and Confidence Building

*"Free your mind, let it all go; fear, doubt, disbelief."*
—Morpheus to Neo ("Mr. Anderson") in the *Matrix*

This chapter specifies training strategies that players can practice to effectively combat information and sequencing errors so that they can automatically execute the skills needed at game-time—thus, freeing their minds. These same strategies can be utilized to combat other mental, emotional, and inspirational performance barriers. Refer to earlier chapters that included questions that could be used to assess performance barriers and mental mechanical problems.

Strategies addressed in this chapter include tough thinking and talking and confidence/trust training. Other strategies—intensity mastery/training, concentration training, and physical/mental preparation and readiness—are addressed in Chapters 13 and 14. These strategies are not only clearly defined, but specific activities and examples for implementing these strategies are also included for easy application by coaches and players.

# Tough Thinking and Talking

Being able to "master" inner dialogue and thoughts takes more than just "thinking positively." How players (and coaches) think and talk to themselves can enhance or hurt performances. Those athletes who are more aware of their thoughts and self-talk, and who also develop plans for dealing with inappropriate and damaging thoughts and talk, are more consistent performers and perform better in pressure situations. Thinking and talking tough are two difficult things to do, especially in pressure situations (e.g., speaking in front of a class, playing in a title game, taking exams, taking a penalty kick in the closing minutes of a match).

Tough thinking and talking means having productive thoughts prior to, and during, games. Productive thoughts and talk are defined as those that help players perform better via performance cues such as "soft hands" for goalkeepers or "strike on frame" for strikers. Counter to productive thoughts are the negative, self-defeating ones such as, "I can't play with this team" or "I am not good at headers." Negative thoughts and talk are also referred to as "stinking thinking."

> *"Confidence is the result of what we say to ourselves about what we think about ourselves. Players with confidence program their inner tape with positive self-talk, whereas low-confidence players put anxiety into their minds by using negative self-talk."*
>
> —Bill Beswick (2001),
> Mental Skills Trainer for English Premier Club Derby County (p. 23)

Self-statements and -thoughts serve numerous purposes. First, they help direct attention in terms of what specific cues players find themselves focusing on and whether they are advantageous to performance. Second, a player may use self-dialogue to label himself, his teammates, or his opponents, such as "I am a choker," or "This target player is too big and fast for me to win this dual." Finally, these statements and thoughts are used to judge performances, such as "That was a great diagonal ball." As previously stated, these statements and thoughts can really help or destroy mental toughness and automatic, consistent execution.

# Common Types of Negative Thinking

### Worrying About Future Events

When thoughts are focused too much on the future ("What if... I carelessly lose possession?" or   What if we...lose this game?"), present play will suffer greatly. Attentional capacities are limited, so worrying about future events will leave little attentional capacity for present performance. In most cases, what players worry about, such as not making the play or looking foolish because of a bad mistake, will usually occur due to a self-fulfilling prophecy. Simply stated, a self-fulfilling prophecy is the body following the lead set by thoughts and self-talk. Since thoughts govern action, if a player is thinking that he is going to lose possession, his body and actions will follow suit. However, if this player honestly believes that he is going to have a perfect first touch, unless something changes in the environment, such as a speedy defender closing space or a poor pass from a teammate, he has a much greater chance of succeeding in doing so. So many players sabotage their performances before they even step out onto the pitch.

## Fretting Over Mistakes

Fretting over mistakes means that an individual is playing in the past. Players cannot go back and change what has happened, no matter how much they would like to do so. Players can only learn from the past and move on to the next opportunity. Since attentional capacities are limited, it is important to solely play in the present. Using a refocusing routine after making a mistake will help a player stop replaying the mistake over and over again. Replaying a mistake in this way usually results in the athlete carrying the mistakes to the next play or series of plays. Refocusing routines are covered in more detail in Chapter 14.

## Worrying About the Uncontrollables

Almost everyone worries about things out of their control—the uncontrollables—such as weather, traffic, and long lines in restaurants. Players do the same thing in terms of worrying about not making mistakes, the opponent's play, what coaches are thinking, and outcome. Even an athlete's play during games is an uncontrollable, since he has no control over how the opponent will play. All players can do is to make it as difficult as possible for opponents to play to their fullest potential. Helping players identify what they do and do not have control over is a good place to start. Players (and coaches) need to realize that if they have no control over a situation, they should let it go and refocus on things that they can control, like their preparation and execution. Chapter 13 features a chart that players can complete that will help them acquire this skill.

## Fretting Over Weaknesses During a Game

Ideally, while competing, players should be on "automatic" and simply read and react to the ever-changing game situations. This state tends to be the signature of most top players—they play better when they just play. Yet, many players really struggle with "freeing the mind" and just playing. If players need to have a couple of thoughts or statements in their heads, ensure that they are productive in nature. Productive thoughts and self-talk should include technical or strategic cues that help players play better, such as "Get into the near post space quicker on the next corner," or "The keeper cheats off his line, so strike the next shot high," or even motivational talk, such as "Let that one go and get ready for the next pass." If players are thinking and evaluating about how poorly they are playing, they will only play worse. Maintaining either a clear mind or using productive cues is not easy. It takes practice.

## Focusing Too Much on Winning

Despite the fact that most players compete to win, when it becomes the sole reason for playing they are setting themselves up for failure. Players and coaches must understand that winning is a process, and that if players don't work on the process of playing well, winning will not happen unless the team gets lucky or plays against a lesser opponent. Players should be thinking of ways to play better and help the team rather than just about winning the game. Also, opponents have a lot to do with whether teams win or not, so winning is somewhat of an uncontrollable. Coaches can begin to change this mindset by stressing game execution ("How are we going to win?") rather than simply on beating the opponent.

Figure 12-1. Winning consistently requires a focus on the process and the team.

### Fretting Over Being Perfect

Another uncontrollable is trying to be perfect. No one is that good, and so much is beyond players' control. *Striving* to be perfect is a sign of a true competitor, but *expecting* to be perfect is a sign of inappropriate and irrational thinking that sets an athlete up for failure on a daily basis. This type of thinking can also erode motivation and confidence.

# Techniques to Develop Tough Thinking and Talking

Being a tough thinker and talker takes practice. Players can use exercises such as awareness training, thought stopping, restructuring, visualizing, and self-coaching statements to help improve in this area. Each of these techniques is addressed later in this chapter.

Do your players know what works for them versus what does not work for them? To test them, have them complete Figure 12-2. Those who are unaware of what works for them (who cannot identify these simple, self-reflections) are at a disadvantage, because they first need to improve upon their awareness abilities before sharpening the mental skills. Players who at least know some of what they are thinking and saying prior to, during, and after play are in a position to change their mindset to productives rather than negatives. When athletes think about negative things and get down on themselves, they usually play their worst games. On the other hand, players who keep thinking productively and find ways to feel composed end up having their better performances. Thinking productively is easy when a player is playing well; it is a different story when things are not going so well. It is called mental toughness for a reason. It is tough to think this way consistently, especially in tougher times, when things are not going the athlete's way.

Once players have identified the most common negative thoughts and self-statements they say to themselves before and during games, and they replace them with productive thoughts and self-statements, the next step entails believing in the productive statements and not the negative ones. Players do this by "building a case" for why these productive thoughts and self-statements are true.

- Example 1: "I really am a good player because I made this top team and I play a lot."
- Example 2: "I want to be the player with the ball at my feet in the final minutes because I have done so in the past and won the game with a big play."
- Example 3: "My coach and teammates will still respect me even if I make mistakes."
- Example 4: "I don't have to worry about making mistakes, because everyone makes mistakes and they are necessary to become the best player I can be."

| Identify the most common negative thoughts that enter into your head before/during games | Identify the most common negative self-statements you say to yourself before/during games |
|---|---|
| (1) | (1) |
| (2) | (2) |
| (3) | (3) |
| (4) | (4) |
| List a productive thought to replace the negative statement listed above | List a productive self-statement to replace the negative statement listed above |
| (1) | (1) |
| (2) | (2) |
| (3) | (3) |
| (4) | (4) |

Figure 12-2. Identifying tough thoughts and talk

Keep in mind that some athletes can be pretty good about keeping themselves positive and productive, but even these athletes need to work on their mental toughness and mechanics. In times of big-time pressure (e.g., championship game, big exam, penalty kick), players who have not practiced these skills may choke under pressure if they've begun to listen and believe the negative thoughts and talk that have seeped in.

# Confidence and Trust Training

Confidence is an inner belief that certain tasks can be accomplished. Top performers from all sports have been found to be very confident about their performances. They do not doubt their abilities, but rather believe that every time out on the court or field they can and will play well. Players who are able to think this way do not let their play dictate their confidence. Instead, their confidence level remains high and consistent, thereby dictating their performance (e.g., high confidence equals top performance).

Confidence is similar to trust. Athletes who trust their abilities do not doubt their physical, technical, and tactical skills or their mental mechanics, because they know that that in times of need (big play), they will perform and these skills will get the job done. When athletes begin to lose trust in their abilities, via negative talk or thoughts, their levels of anxiety and muscle tension increase. An overnarrowing of attention causes some players to miss important performance cues. Some athletes will even change their mechanics in an attempt to get back on track, such as forcing plays, or aiming or controlling their passes or swings. The concept of trust and its impact on mechanical changes is discussed later in this section, along with strategies to combat this occurrence.

Confidence has been described as an "inverted U" process. As Figure 12-3 indicates, most players do not perform optimally when their level of confidence is low, yet as their confidence increases, so does the level of play. Unfortunately, once their confidence heightens to a level of "overconfidence," performance will begin to wane. Players who begin to assume that they will come up with great plays at will are the same ones who stop doing what they did to achieve their level of success (e.g., worked hard, focused on the process, led the team through solid play and encouragement). Arrogance often replaces the "little things," the intangibles that helped these players achieve. When the time comes that the successes are not as common, these same players may turn on coaches and teammates (i.e., blame them for his failures) and drift further away from the "ingredients" that made them stand out and succeed. Players who are able to maintain a consistently high level of confidence, regardless of performance outcome, are giving themselves the best chance to succeed come game time.

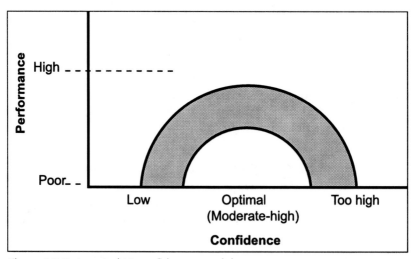

Figure 12-3. Inverted U confidence model

To assist those players in need of improving their confidence, have them begin the process by completing the lists in Figure 12-4. Next, have players come up with statements that reflect these same positive attitudes and thoughts about themselves and their abilities. These positive statements are referred to as self-coaching statements and should express personal, sometimes motivating, messages. Figure 12-5 offers a chart in which to record these statements. Some examples include the following:

- "I really come through in pressure situations. I am our team's go-to player!"
- "I'm the one who really wants the ball when the game is on the line."
- "I love playing in big games."
- "I feel like I can come up with a big play in any situation."

| Positive Qualities | Successes |
|---|---|
| (1) | (1) |
| (2) | (2) |
| (3) | (3) |
| (4) | (4) |
| (5) | (5) |

Figure 12-4. Confidence-building statements

| Self-Coaching Statements |
|---|
| * |
| * |
| * |
| * |
| * |
| * |
| * |

Figure 12-5. Self-coaching statement chart

Now that the players have some feel-good, productive, and motivating self-coaching statements, what do they do with them? Players should find creative ways to use them as often as possible. Consider the following examples of how players can make the most of the statements that work best for them. You can suggest that players:

- Choose one or two statements each day to repeat over and over, especially prior to playing.
- Write the statement on paper many times throughout the day, with the idea in mind that the more that they tell themselves these statements, the more they will really believe them.
- Post these statements in a folder to read over when they have a few spare moments.
- Post them somewhere in their room so that they see them many times throughout the day.
- Write them down and put them in their sport bags, so that they can review them before and after practices or games as they put on their equipment and uniforms.
- Record the statements on audiotape or compact disc, along with some of their favorite music, and play them whenever they can, especially before practice and games.
- Visualize highlights from past successful performances or mentally picture future match play.

Taking advantage of the many sources of performance confidence can be a tremendous way to optimize player confidence. Coaches should attempt to refer to these many sources when they address their players. For example, during pregame talks, coaches can highlight their players' preparation (watching the tape of the opponent), emphasize the use of an individual and/or team highlight tape (previous success), remind players that they have run the scouting tactics and set pieces all week (mastery), and have organized pregame routines to follow (mental preparation). The following sources of confidence have been identified by Robin Vealey, a sport psychology researcher (2002):

- Previous accomplishments—watching previous successes on video
- Vicarious experience—gaining confidence and energy by watching teammates' successes or watching or reading about the accomplishments of athletes from other sports
- Communication—openly and honestly communicating goes a long way in helping players and teammates feel appreciated and valued.
- Physical presentation—looking the part (outside-in training) and not showing what is really going on inside
- Physical preparation—working as hard as possible in training and conditioning
- Mental preparation—realizing the importance of the mental game and doing something about it via establishing routines and different forms of preparation, readiness, and coping

- Situational favorableness—gaining something positive and motivating from the site of the competition; for example, playing well there last time, or a good "look" or "feel" about it
- Leadership—a sense that when it comes to "crunch time," the team leaders, coaches, or captains will lead the way
- Mastery attempts—appreciating efforts at improving the overall game and acknowledging successes in these areas; attempting to improve upon yesterday's performance
- Quality training—knowing the difference between quality training sessions and going through the motions, and then actively ensuring that quality sessions prevail

In addition to utilizing these sources of confidence in their feedback to players, coaches should make players aware of these sources and attempt to utilize them pre- and postgame. Players who are able to leave practices, and especially games, with several "kudos," or things that they did well (i.e., positive feedback received from

Courtesy of UMASS Sports Information

Figure 12-6. Coaches can greatly improve player confidence by utilizing the many sources of confidence during and after practice and game play.

coaches and teammates), will increase their level of internal confidence. Most competitive athletes leave games thinking about and harping on their mistakes and bad moments of play. Teaching players to learn from these errors and leave them behind will make them better prepared, more confident, and ready for the next practice and game. Additionally, players should be encouraged to "deposit" this confidence-enhancing feedback into their internal confidence base by writing it down or reciting it as a pregame routine. Maintaining an optimal level of confidence in good times and in bad takes conscious work. As stated previously, thinking in this fashion is not easy, which is why it is called mental "toughness."

To aid in practice and game preparation, as well as to improve confidence on a daily basis, players should utilize *mental visualization.* The skill technique is described in detail in Chapter 13, along with a tutorial. In brief, visualization involves using as many senses as possible to view and feel sporting images prior to actually performing them on the pitch. If visualization is performed correctly, the images are vivid, in color, and in total control. Images should be positively viewed, with great details included, to make it as real as possible. The more real the image, the more the image and action are viewed, and the more emotion that is interjected into the scene, the more experience the performer will have with the particular skill or game-related situation. The player will have "been there, done that" literally hundreds of times. So if players struggle playing a particular position, or have difficulty grasping complex tactics, practicing seeing themselves perform correctly will aid in learning and performing, and will greatly enhance confidence levels.

*"Of great importance is the link between visualization—how we see ourselves—and our emotional state, our energy state, and therefore our potential for performance. As we exercise the mind it grows stronger. The more the player pictures success, the more energy he or she creates to achieve it."*
—Bill Beswick, Mental Skills Trainer for English Premier Club Derby County
(2001, p. 78-79)

What I have advised for most of my soccer-playing clients is to pass, kick, score, or save 50 to 100 balls a night. Therefore, these players are "practicing" away from the practice field—albeit in their mind's eye—the skills that are in need of improvement. Some players have gone the extra mile and have a picture of a goal next to their bed, and they imagine scoring 50 goals each night, from different serves and angles—a lot of goals scored in a week's time! Defenders can envision breaking up plays or heading the ball away on crosses; midfielders can replay their different possessions during the last game, and keepers can make hundreds of saves without ever hitting the ground! Bill Beswick, the mental-skill trainer for one of England's top clubs, reports that "The more a player practices visualization, the more accurate the images will become. The memory trace will become stronger, the image more accessible, and the emotional support more powerful, boosting both motivation and confidence" (p. 70). Visualization can be used to not only enhance confidence, but also to improve preparation and readiness, skill learning, and tactical awareness; manage stress; improve concentration; regulate energy/emotional levels; and enhance recovery from setbacks, mistakes, and injuries. Visualization is a very powerful skill for every player to practice and master.

# Chapter Summary

- Those athletes who are more aware of their thoughts and self-talk, and who also develop plans for dealing with inappropriate and damaging thoughts and talk, are more consistent performers and perform better in pressure situations.
- Common types of negative, self-defeating talk include worrying about future events, fretting over mistakes, worrying about the uncontrollables, fretting over the present level of play, focusing too much on winning, and having an expectation of playing perfectly.
- When athletes begin to lose trust in their abilities, via negative talk or thoughts, their levels of anxiety and muscle tension increase. An overnarrowing of attention causes some players to miss important performance cues.
- Coaches should utilize the many sources of confidence in their feedback and teaching, including previous successes, physical presentation, mental and physical preparation, leadership endeavors, mastery attempts, and quality practice.

# 13

# Training for Automaticity V: Combating Mental Barriers— Mastering Intensity Control and Attentional Focus

The ability to handle pressure, and the emotional reaction to pressure, is referred to as intensity control. Gaining control and mastery over intensity is one of the most important things players and coaches can do to improve upon their practice and game readiness. Levels of intensity are very specific to each athlete. Some athletes perform better when they have low levels of intensity (very relaxed), others need a moderate level (a composed intensity), and still others need a high level of intensity (wired).

Once in their state of optimal intensity, players become more motivated, confident, focused, and ready. To determine what the optimal intensity is, each player should determine what works best for him. Have players think in terms of three distinct components:

- What do you *feel* physically (tense muscles, rapid breathing, rapid heart rate)?
- What are your *behaviors* before games? Some players like to sit by themselves and listen to tunes, some like to hang with teammates, and others like to buzz around the locker room and pace.
- What do you *think* about prior to a match? Or prior to taking a set-piece or corner? Are you worried about how you or the team will play or are you thinking confidently? Are you too focused on the outcome (winning), or do you focus on the process of playing your game?

Players who are aware of what works for them will be better able to control their intensity levels, especially in pressure-packed situations, than those players who don't have a clue about their mental and emotional states. One way that players can improve their awareness is by completing the following checklist, which lists common reactions to overintensity. Players are asked to put a check mark next to the symptoms they commonly experience.

# Overintensity

## Symptoms of Overintensity

- Physical:

    _____ muscle tension

    _____ shortened breathing

    _____ excessive sweating

    _____ nausea

    _____ cold extremities

    _____increase in blood pressure and heart rate

- Behavioral:

    _____ increase in pace during competition

    _____ bracing muscles (e.g., shoulders up to the ears)

    _____ increase in superstitious behaviors

    _____ quickly agitated

    _____ loss of coordination

    _____ choke in performance or evaluative situations

- Mental:

    _____ negative self-talk and thoughts

    _____ irrational thinking

    _____ overnarrowing of concentration

    _____ inability to let go of mistakes

    _____ feeling of uncontrollability

- Emotional:

_____ feeling of fear of making mistakes, embarrassment, or letting others down

## Causes of Overintensity

- A lack of confidence ("stinkin' thinking" and self-talk)
- A focus on the outcome (winning), or on being the best player on the field rather than enjoying the process
- A tendency to crack under the weight of the expectations of others—namely parents, teammates, or coaches—or of unrealistic goals
- An unfamiliarity with certain situations and places, such as arriving late to the game site, or playing a new role or a new system
- Unexpected events, like having to play with a cold, with a nagging injury, or without the team leader
- Continual worry over the uncontrollables, or those things that most people believe that they have control over, but, in reality, do not. For example, some athletes get so worried about what their coaches think of them that it distracts them and could adversely affect their play.

An exercise to help players enhance their awareness of what they do and do not have control over is presented in Figure 13-1. It is important for athletes to not waste valuable mental energy and limited attentional capacity on worrying or fretting over those things that are beyond their immediate control. Athletes who are prone to this excess concern over the uncontrollables will have a decreased sense of control, waning confidence, and overintensity issues.

| Controllables | Uncontrollables |
|---|---|
| Ex. 1: my workrate at practice | Ex. 1: calls made by officials |
| Ex. 2: if not pleased with something, can go and talk to coach | Ex. 2: decisions regarding playing time and play calling by my coach |
| * | * |
| * | * |
| * | * |
| * | * |
| * | * |
| * | * |

Figure 13-1. The controllables and the uncontrollables

# Underintensity

When players struggle with being underintense for games, their performances can suffer as well. Underintensity is characterized by low energy levels, little motivation and drive, and an attentional focus that is so broad that important performance cues go unnoticed. The symptoms of underintensity can include the following:

- Physical—lethargy; low heart rate (resting heart rate); low energy
- Behavioral—decrease in "sharpness" during play; looking "slow" and being a "step too late"; poor performance
- Mental—react more to distractions; loss of motivation to give maximal effort; difficulty narrowing attentional focus to the important details of performing and the opponents

## Causes of Underintensity

- Fatigue from a lack of rest and recovery between games, practices, school, and social activities
- Sleeping difficulties
- Poor eating/nutritional habits
- Lack of adequate hydration
- Nagging injuries left untreated
- Lack of motivation and drive (e.g., playing an opponent that the team has beaten numerous times before)
- Overconfidence, such as, "We can beat this team on our worst day."

Overconfidence is one reason why upsets happen all the time in sport, because players begin to feel that they can put in "half effort" and still accomplish the outcome (winning). This attitude is one of the biggest problems associate with a team that is too outcome-oriented. A process-oriented team will attempt to improve upon its last performance, regardless of the opponent. It has been said that the "great ones," including Jordan, Tiger, Gretzky, Montana, Clemens, Rice, Elway, Donovan, and Beckenbauer, were or are driven to perform better than they did the game before. What a tough challenge for these truly exceptional competitors!

# Strategies to Decrease Intensity

Mastering intensity levels entails being able to lower intensity levels when athletes perceive that they are too amped and excited, as well as being able to increase intensity levels when they are bored or unmotivated. When players struggle with overintensity, assist them with the following strategies.

## Understanding the Causes of Overintensity

The first question that players should attempt to answer is how these feelings of overintensity affect their feelings, thoughts, and performances. Some athletes tend to get "too much in their heads" (mental) by getting so negative about their games, while others tend to get overly "tight and tense," signaling physical tension in places that can adversely affect performance. Very few soccer skills can be performed well when the muscles are tensed up. Other athletes experience a combination of these effects. To maximize effectiveness at lowering intensity levels to an optimal level, ensure that if players are "too much in the head," they incorporate mental strategies, but if players are too "tight and tense," they practice physical relaxation strategies. Players who experience a combination of the two should incorporate strategies from both categories. Performance strategies are included so that coaches can better assist their players with their handling of intensity.

## Physical Strategies

Releasing tension with a physical warm-up routine followed by stretching can be quite beneficial. Practicing tension-relaxation cycles is also advisable to educate players on distinguishing the differences between feelings of relaxation and tension. In down times, such as before going to bed or before practice, making a fist tight (tension) and then releasing and opening up the fingers and feeling the tension run out of the fingers will help to clarify feelings of relaxation. Have players continue this cycle numerous times until the hands feel totally relaxed after the tension cycle. This tension-relaxation cycle can be conducted with any muscle group that harbors muscle tension.

It does take practice to self-induce relaxation during games, so it is recommended that athletes take some time every day to practice the technique. Some elite athletes prefer to do a head-to-toe tension-relaxation cycle, moving from one muscle group to the next, in what is referred to as progressive relaxation. The more aware players are of the feelings of tension and relaxation, the quicker they can release the tension in the heat of competition.

The next skill strategy used to regulate intensity levels is breathing. When players are extremely anxious and/or tense, they may respond to this intensity with shortened, irregular breathing patterns. Without adequate oxygen, players become fatigued, because the cardiovascular and muscular systems do not work as efficiently as is needed, and performance is thereby affected.

*"Before an important shot, I relax myself by taking a long, deep breath."*
—Tiger Woods (2001, p. 265)

It is very important that athletes replenish their oxygen supply, simply by inhaling through the nose for a four-count. The belly should push out as a sign that enough air in being inhaled and that it is getting deep enough into the lungs. Have players exhale through the mouth for a four-count, as they focus on feeling any tension in the muscles and body with each exhaled breath. Some athletes will tense a muscle group with each inhalation, and then relax the muscle on each exhalation for a combined relaxation effect.

## Mental Strategies

If players feel anxious prior to game time, it is important for them to discontinue focusing on their debilitating thoughts and self-dialogue. Rather, encourage players to engage in conversations with teammates or listen to music, which will provide a much-needed distraction. Once these feelings have subsided, players can begin to prepare for the upcoming game. Coaches must allow for individual pregame time, because every player differs in how he gets himself ready. If players are not given their own time, it could lead to more anxiety and counteract the coach's methods for getting the team "up" and ready for games. Most coaches allow at least 30 minutes for player pregame time.

Another strategy for coaches to try is to avoid telling players during games to "relax." If players do not know how to relax, this statement will hurt rather than help them. What occurs in some situations is that once athletes hear that command, they get even more anxious because they think that they must be emitting some obvious "nervous behaviors" to prompt their coach to yell that out to them. One of the first things that players can do to alleviate these threatening thoughts or anxieties is to try to perceive the impending situation or competition as nonthreatening. This skill is called *reframing.* Instead of thinking of the upcoming game as an extremely nerve-racking situation, player can view it instead as a challenge. What normally accompanies negative perceptions are negative thoughts, avoidance thoughts and practices (just wanting to get it over with or skipping out), or negative feelings and tight muscles.

Being a competitor means embracing situations in which players have to be at their best to succeed. Teaching players to seek out challenges rather than escape from potentially stressful situations is valuable. Enabling players to stay productive and positive instead of turning negative ("I can't play well against this team") can really go a long way. It is a lot easier said than done, however. The key is for players to be aware of when they are turning negative with their thoughts and self-dialogue—and then stop. Replacing these negative, self-defeating thoughts and talk with productive comments ("I played well last week, so there should be no reason why I can't bring my 'A' game against these guys") can help players change their current way of thinking and become consistent, productive thinkers. It is advisable for players to write down their most common negative thoughts and self-talk, and then replace them with productive statements (see Figure 12-1). After repeating this process for several weeks, players will begin to utilize more productive statements. If negative thoughts break through, they will be replaced with helpful, constructive comments.

## Performance Strategies

Coaches should promote familiarity with game situations by attempting to simulate game conditions and specific game situations in practice. Preparing for all of the unexpected situations that could arise before and during games is a valuable exercise for coaches and players.

Coaches and players must also keep errors in proper perspective. Once players begin to worry about the negative consequences of their mistakes, which could include verbal harassment by coaches, fans, or parents, they will begin to press, aim, and control their movements. All of these actions are potentially detrimental to optimal, consistent performance.

Coaches who avoid overemphasizing outcome (winning, records, "must-win" situations) to their players will help them to stay more process- focused (e.g., working toward improving their play rather than on just getting the result). Chapters 15 and 16 go into greater detail about coaching with a process focus. As mentioned earlier, players can only control their own effort and play, not the play of others, so winning is somewhat of an uncontrollable. A team may have their best outing of the season, yet still lose due to a bad officiating call, unlucky bounces, or any one of hundreds of incidents that could stand in the way of the win. What is most productive for players is to emphasize the process, or what they need to do prior to, during, and after plays to help lead their team down the field.

This "process" approach helps players focus on one play at a time. Sometimes players need to adopt a "fake it until you make it" attitude to be able to move past a poor play or run of bad bounces or missed tackles. In pressure situations, when players may become quite nervous (e.g., several mistakes in a row, taking a penalty kick), acting and looking cool, calm, and composed can get translated by the "software" (i.e., brain impulses, thoughts, muscles) as meaning that everything is alright, so players can simply go for it. This technique has been referred to as *outside-in training* (Loehr, 1994). Players do something on the outside, such as physical presentation, acting, and behaviors that gets translated as a good thing on the inside via thoughts and emotions. One of the simplest strategies players and coaches can use on the "outside" that has an unbelievable effect on the "inside" is smile. Smiling releases chemicals into the system that are linked to feelings of happiness and relaxation.

Finally, *inside-out training* (Loehr, 1994) occurs when players think productively and positively about their ability and their chances of success on the inside, which gets translated by the body as a positive, energizing message. This process sharpens the outside performance, such as endurance, strength on the ball, reaction time, speed of play, and power in the air, to function optimally. The strategies contained in this book feature both outside-in (physical toughness and technical training) and inside-out (mental, emotional toughness) training programs.

# Strategies to Increase Intensity

When players are not amped enough and are in need of a jump start, numerous ways of increasing intensity levels are available.

## Physical Strategies

Intense activity, such as a sharp pregame warm-up, is one of the most effective physical strategies to employ when the team is just lethargic. Physical activity that is sport-specific is desirable, but in the off-season, cross-training activities, such as playing other sports or performing different conditioning activities, can be very beneficial. "Fake it until you make it" can help in this case as well. Acting as if they are totally invested in the upcoming game not only may help the team get more "into it," but it may also have the same effect on each individual player.

## Mental Strategies

Having players listen to their favorite upbeat tunes can help get them more "into" practice, lifting, conditioning, or game play. Another strategy that is widely used by elite athletes from most sports is the use of *mental imagery*. Imagery, also termed visualization, has been mentioned several times in this book because this skill strategy can be used to increase confidence, motivation, preparation, and readiness, and control intensity levels. Utilizing mental imagery can be very effective in improving drive and energy, especially when a player visualizes energizing images and past performance accomplishments. A quick-reference tutorial on imagery, found in Figure 13-2, will assist players in getting started with this skill strategy.

Players can visualize performing a skill or replay a particular event in one of two ways. From an *internal perspective,* the skill is viewed from inside the "mind's eye." For example players should actually see and feel the ball at their feet or in their hands (for keepers). When using this type of imagery, the brain is sending messages to the muscles as if the player is actually passing, heading, shooting, or making a save on a in-swinging crossed ball. From an *external perspective,* players watch themselves as a spectator would, or watch themselves play on television or video. Internal imagery is believed to be more effective according to some research, although the external approach is still effective at helping improve confidence, motivation, and anxiety and intensity regulation.

## Imagery Tutorial

Step 1: Go to a quiet place where you can relax and not be disturbed.

Step 2: Select a variety of scenes and develop them with rich detail, including colors, sounds, smells, and feelings if possible (your bedroom, favorite class, scenes of your dog playing...).

Step 3: Select sport-specific images and include as much detail as possible.

Step 4: Practice visualizing people (teammates, fans, parents) into the scenes.

Step 5: Imagine being in a specific sport situation, either in the past (replay), or in a future event. Bring in as much detail as possible. Also feel yourself experiencing success in these scenes.

Step 6: When you get proficient at your visualization, you can then try to replay negative events so you can edit them the way you really wanted them to turn out. Being able to fix these negative events may help in ensuring that they don't get repeated, while also helping to increase confidence and decrease anxiety about these specific sport situations.

Step 7: It is highly recommended that you visually practice specific sport skills and game-related situations, especially those that may be giving you some problems, as often as possible.

Figure 13-2. Imagery tutorial

One final exercise can assist players in finding their optimal intensity zone (Figure 13-3). As mentioned earlier, some players perform better when they have high levels of intensity, others prefer moderate levels, and some operate better at lower levels. To help players find their zone, which represents the perfect level of intensity for them, have them rate and record their pregame intensity level from 1 (not intense at all) to 10 (highest intensity). The next step is to have them rate their performance after each game from 1 (played awful) to 10 (ESPN highlight!). After monitoring a few games, players should be able to see a pattern, and discover the right level of intensity for them to perform at their best.

| Pre-game Intensity Level | Performance Rating |
|---|---|
| game 1 = | game 1 = |
| game 2 = | game 2 = |
| game 3 = | game 3 = |
| game 4 = | game 4 = |
| game 5 = | game 5 = |
| Describe what your zone is like. | Zone =_____ |
| Describe your feelings, thoughts, behaviors. | |

Figure 13-3. Finding the intensity zone

# Attentional Focus and Competitive Concentration

The majority of coaches have players who struggle with intensity issues and who have difficulty keeping their attentional focus on what is really important. Similar to the scenario mentioned earlier with perceived tension/anxiety, it is common to hear coaches yell out to players "stay focused out there" or—another favorite—"keep your head in the game." Without realizing it, while these coaches are identifying the problem, they are also contributing more pressure and stress, which only makes the player's focus even worse. This statement is especially true for those players who thought that they were really focusing, but since the coach said something to the contrary, they then think that the coach must have seen something indicating that their concentration is truly "off."

The following are some important terms in understanding attentional focus. Figure 13-5 (Nideffer, 1976; 1989) depicts the many types of attentional focus.
- Attentional focus—an athlete's ability to focus on the most relevant information during play
- Concentration—the mental skills involved in keeping the focus on the most relevant performance cues
- Attentional style—the preferred style of focusing on the sport environment

Courtesy of Dartmouth Sports Information

Figure 13-4. Attending to the proper cues around and off the ball is a very important mental skill for all players on the pitch, especially midfielders.

- Attentional switching—the ability to adjust attentional focus, width, and direction, depending upon what is required in certain situations
  - ✓ Width of attention—can range on a continuum
  - ✓ Narrowing—focus is on a small number of cues
  - ✓ Broadening—focus is on several different cues
- Direction of attention—either the focus is internal or external (cannot be both)
  - ✓ Internal—focus is directed inward, toward thoughts and feelings
  - ✓ External—focus is directed outward, into the environment (e.g., on defensive coverages or opponent runs/off ball movement)

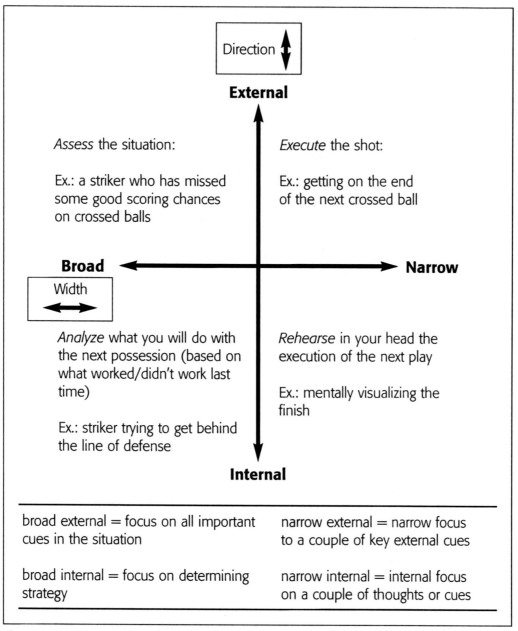

Figure 13-5. Components of attentional focus

## Concentration Training

To be effective at "freeing the mind," players must be able to foster adequate attention and concentration control. Doing so requires the ability to focus and switch attention as needed during pressure situations. The following strategies can assist players in executing automatically and effectively.

This process begins with the evaluation of attentional strengths and weaknesses via the Offensive and Defensive Mental Skills Questionnaire presented in Chapter 4. Identify the important components of attention, including width (narrow or broad), direction (internal or external), and attentional switching.

Next, coaches can identify the attentional demands of soccer and of specific positions (Figure 13-6) (Schmidt, Peper, & Wilson, 2001). Helping players realize the attentional demands of certain situations can assist them in focusing on the most relevant cues in an organized fashion. Those coaches who attend to the minute details of the game most likely teach their players these important attentional cues. Once players are armed with this information, they can simply focus on these relevant cues prior to execution, thus eliminating the distracting and harmful negative thoughts and self-talk and freeing themselves to play automatically. The next section, "Physical/Mental Preparation and Readiness," describes how these attentional components can be organized, prior to playing as pregame routines or during play as execution routines.

| Sport Situation | Attentional Demands | | | |
| | Broad | | Narrow | |
| | Internal | External | Internal | External |
| --- | --- | --- | --- | --- |
| Ex. 1: a sweeper deciding to stay in cover position or step up to challenge the ball | How did I cover it last time? | Location of the ball and the most danger-ous option | Focus on the ball and on delaying the attack | Ball winning! |
| Ex. 2: keeper on a crossed ball | Fastest way to the ball | Quick call and attack the ball | Focus only on ball contact | Ball winning! |
| | | | | |

Figure 13-6. Attentional demands of positional play

Assessing the most common concentration problems in soccer is another good strategy that coaches can utilize while teaching specific technical points (Figure 13-7) (Nideffer, 1976; Ziegler, 2002). For players to be in control of their thoughts and emotions before each ball contact, it is important that they are aware of their thoughts and feelings, as well as the specific cues that they should be attending to and the ones that they should eliminate. Having an attentional focus that is too narrow-internal, for example, at the wrong time could confuse the player due to focusing on inappropriate cues (internal distractions), rather than on cues in the environment (e.g., location of weakside attackers, number of covering defenders).

| Attentional Style | Benefits to Using | Cost to Using   Mistakes due to… |
|---|---|---|
| Broad external | good awareness of environment | …attending to distracting sport cues (Ex.: bad call from ref; crowd noise) |
| Broad internal | good planning-strategic thinking | …overanalysis = thinking too much (Ex.: hesitation; apprehension) |
| Narrow external | can effectively lock in on a couple of cues | …too narrow = miss critical cues (Ex.: too focused on player or ball) |
| Narrow internal | good at locking in on a single thought | …could *choke* = too internal (Ex.: too much in head = negativity) |

Figure 13-7. Cost-benefit to attentional styles

Be aware of other variables that can impact players' abilities to control their attentional capacities. It is important to realize the relationship between intensity and attention. Players who become overly tense and anxious will have a difficult time keeping their focus on the important cues. Some players will keep switching from internal to external stimuli, which will lead to overload and confusion. An athlete could lose confidence, which will further increase anxiety and tension, and worsen performance. Some players, when in the face of adversity and increased pressure or anxiety, will fall back on their most preferred attentional style, which may be wrong for the particular situation. Anxiety and tension can also cause difficulties in properly switching from one attentional style to another (direction and width).

Internal and external distractions are also of concern. Figure 13-8 lists pertinent sources of distractions, both internal and external (Voight, 2000b).

One of the major ways in which distractions affect performance is by consuming limited attentional capacities. Instead of using attentional resources for focusing on the necessary performance cues—physical, technical, strategic, or mental cues—players wastefully attend to distractions, which either do nothing to aid performance or cause performances to suffer. Attending to distractions also evokes *psychological* reactions, such as negative, depreciating thoughts, worry, or uncertainty; *physiological* reactions, such as tense muscles, shallow breathing, or rigid movements; or *emotional* reactions, such as anger, frustration, or a loss of control. Conversely, these responses can take

| Internal Distractions | External Distractions |
|---|---|
| • focus on irrelevant performance cues | • media coverage |
| • inability to switch attention from one play to another | • interviews with media |
| | • presence of family and friends |
| • focus on past mistakes or future concerns | • presence of a mass of fans who may have traveled from afar |
| • worry over outcome | • spectator distractions during play |
| • fear of failure | • visual distractions |
| • inability to "quiet the mind"; being too much "in the head" | • auditory distractions |
| | • verbal abuse |
| • negative self-talk | • pressure from boosters, administrators to win (benefits to school) |
| • worry over expectations of others | • seeding/ranking |
| • indecision during play (lack of trust/confidence) | • playing a "giant killer" |
| | • playing on the road |
| • "what if" statements | • playing at home |
| • uncertainty | • previous performance against opponent |
| • selfish thinking | |

Figure 13-8. Internal and external distractions

many athletes off their top games. They are not only a waste of time and effort, but these responses can definitely have an adverse effect on preparation and performance.

A third way in which distractions affect performance is through the narrowing of attentional focus, which causes *choking*. When players get too negative, worried, or anxious, their focus narrows as they attend to less of what they should be focusing on. This response causes critical cues that are necessary for effective execution to be blocked out. Blocking out the cues can cause some players to miss easy plays, make poor passes, get caught watching the wrong cues, or make hundreds of other dysfunctional plays.

Chapter 14 delves into greater detail of how to incorporate these attentional dimensions into preparatory and execution routines. Utilizing preparatory and execution routines to better organize the time prior to the next touch on the ball can incorporate the numerous mental-skill training strategies already discussed. Soccer players and teams should keep the following anecdote in mind the next time a coach tells the team to "play the full match, until the final whistle." Bayern Munich was playing Manchester United in the 1999 European Club Championship. As the game entered into the ninetieth minute, Bayern Munich was winning 1-0, and it appeared that the players began their celebrations a couple of minutes too soon (one player waved to a fan in the crowd). Manchester United, who played until the final whistle sounded, seized the moment and scored two goals in the final three minutes to win with a remarkable comeback effort! As stated by Bill Beswick (2001), "For Bayern, it was truly a case of 99 percent concentration not being enough in a major final" (p. 52).

Figure 13-9. The crowd, especially one in Manchester, England, could be a major distraction for some players and teams.

# Chapter Summary

- Gaining control and mastery over intensity is one of the most important things that players and coaches can do to improve upon their practice and game readiness.
- Causes of overintensity can include low confidence levels, a focus on outcome, expectations, uncertainty and unfamiliarity, and continual worry about uncontrollable events and situations.
- Letdowns in sport are primarily due to being underintense for matches due to playing an inferior opponent, fatigue, improper preparation, nagging injuries, and overconfidence.
- To maximize effectiveness at lowering intensity levels to an optimal level, ensure that if players are "too much in the head," they incorporate mental strategies, but if players are too "tight and tense," they practice physical relaxation strategies.
- Helping players realize the attentional demands of certain situations can assist them in focusing on the most relevant cues in an organized fashion.
- Some players, in the face of adversity and increased pressure or anxiety, will fall back on their most preferred attentional style, which may be wrong for the particular situation.
- Each attentional dimension is valuable, as long as players engage the right dimension for the right situation.

# 14

# Training for Automaticity VI: Combating Mental and Inspirational Barriers— Physical/Mental Preparation and Inspirational Strategies

One of the most important factors contributing to top performance is the ability to generate and maintain optimal readiness prior to competition. At the elite level, where athletes possess similar sport-specific and physical abilities, the way that athletes engage their thoughts and emotions before a competition could be the difference between winning and losing. Two methods used to improve physical, mental, and emotional readiness are the use of pre-performance and execution routines. *Pre-performance* and *execution routines* typically consist of thought components such as concentration, productive thoughts, and self-talk; behavioral elements such as walk-throughs and individual rituals; and energizing components such as adequate rest, energy, and hydration. This section outlines ways to help players establish comprehensive, yet simple to apply, prepractice and pregame routines that will both encapsulate tough thinking and feeling and appropriate attentional dynamics.

Figure 13-5, which was used to detail attentional components, also represents the stages of an execution routine. These four types of attentional focus can be part of a preparatory routine for all players on the pitch. The following example is a presave routine designed for keepers. First, once the keeper gets into position for the upcoming crossed ball, his attention should be on assessing the situation *(broad external focus)* in terms of defensive coverage and ball placement, spacing to goal line, and the pace of the through ball. Second, the keeper must analyze the save to be made *(broad internal focus)* and what his primary responsibility is on the play, while also communicating the play ("keeper ball" or "away") to the team. Third, the keeper must prepare himself for the serve *(narrow internal focus)*, giving special attention to focus in on one or two specific cues (thus blocking out distractions and negative thoughts). Once the keeper gets into position, he should be operating on automatic processing *(narrow external focus)*, letting all of his practice, preparation, talent, and skill take over. Thinking is replaced by automatically reacting to what the scene and situation dictate, thus resulting in a dangerous crossed ball being effectively punched out of danger and triggering a counterattack for his team. These attentional processes occur in split seconds, and more experienced keepers make the right decisions at the right times due to continual awareness and quality practice. Coaches should walk young goalkeepers through these attentional processes so that they can make the best skill-execution decisions based on what they perceive from the situation, the environment, and the trust the keeper has in his own in abilities. This same sequence could be used prior to taking set pieces, corner kicks, or penalty kicks, as well as prior to receiving a passed ball or challenging for a defensive, attacking header.

Courtesy of USC Sports Information

Figure 14-1. Midfielders must be able to switch their attentional focus to be most effective, because the pressures of time, space, and opposition come from all sides.

A preparatory routine can not only help prepare players for the next play, mentally and emotionally, but it also can be quite beneficial in helping let go of mistakes such as passing errors, mental mistakes, or misreads of defensive coverage. Doing so will enable athletes to play in the present and take one play at a time. Instead of focusing on past mistakes (thinking in the past), players are instructed to focus on the steps of the routine. *Refocusing* routines can also be used to help deal with frustration, worries, negative thoughts, and self-talk during play. By focusing "in" on this routine, players will be blocking "out" potential distractions.

Preparation and readiness for games should begin before suiting up on game night. Having an organized pregame routine can greatly improve a player's ability to free his head by focusing in on critical elements that help him prepare and ready himself. These routines can also guard against distractions, pregame anxieties, and a loss in focus. To truly achieve optimal readiness, athletes must focus their attention on what their specific needs are prior to playing. If these needs are not inherently apparent, have players brainstorm the specifics behind their best and worst performances (Figure 14-2).

| | Best performance | Worst performance |
|---|---|---|
| How did you feel physically? | | |
| How did you feel emotionally? | | |
| What were you thinking? | | |
| What were your behaviors? | | |
| How was your self-talk? What were you saying to yourself? | | |
| How did you deal with distractions? What were those distractions? | | |

Figure 14-2. Brainstorming pregame needs

Upon completion of the "brainstorming" chart, players must determine the differences between the best and worst performances and prioritize what really helped versus what really hurt preparation and performance. Have players insert these items into Figure 14-3.

| What Really *Helped* You? | What Really *Hurt* Your Game? |
|---|---|
| * | * |
| * | * |
| * | * |
| * | * |
| * | * |
| * | * |

Figure 14-3. Prioritizing pregame routine components

Players should then use the listed information to come up with their ideal pregame routine by answering the following questions:

- What physical feelings are needed?
- What emotional needs must be met?
- What thoughts are preferred?
- What behaviors are conducive to optimal preparation?
- What should the self-talk include?
- What is the best way to maintain focus?

Devising the pregame routine then entails prioritizing specific elements based upon the timing leading up to the big event. This information should be broken down as follows:

- 48 hours prior to game time
- 24 hours prior to game time
- The morning of the game
- Two hours before game time
- One hour before game time
- Just prior to the opening whistle

During the flow of play, when players finds themselves struggling to make plays, they should be able to rely on preset *coping routines* to help get back on their game. These coping routines can be executed just prior to their preparatory routine, especially if a player needs to let go of a past mistake. Specific elements that can be included in a coping routine include the following:

- A subtle way of letting go of any pent-up frustration over a past mistake, such as clenching the fist and then releasing the tension, clapping hands, pounding a fist into the other hand, or verbally letting it out without making a spectacle
- Preselected phrases such as "I'm ready," "Forget the mistake," or "Focus on your role," to help focus on the next play while leaving the past play in the past
- Triggers or actions that symbolically "wipe away" the past mistake or distraction; for example, wiping the hands on the shirt so as to wipe the mistake away
- Performance cues as reminders of what needs to be done "right now" to succeed. For example, one or two tactical points can be used, such as "Okay, let's take care of the ball better on this possession," or "Quickly scan the opponents."
- Deep breaths, along with some motivating self-talk to get back into form. A player focusing on the strengths of his game, as well as intently focusing on what needs to be done with the next touch of the ball, will block out distractions while helping him perform past his potential.

Some teams go a bit further and devise *team coping routines* to use when they are having a rough time and momentum is working against them. They are therefore able to stay connected and begin making plays again. Components of the team routine include ensuring that the team stays vocal, always coming together for a "five," especially after conceding a goal, and using teammates' "buttons." These "buttons" refer to what each player needs from his teammates when things are not going his way. For example, some players want their teammates to give them "fives," others want words of encouragement, and others want to be challenged to get the job done. When players are armed with this information, they can step in and say and do the right thing to help their teammate get back into the game. With a large team, each positional unit shares their particular "buttons" with each other. Each back (and keeper), midfielder, and striker knows exactly what to do or say, or what not to do or say, to each positional teammate in case play begins to suffer.

Figure 14-4 lists several "on-the-fly routines" used by the NHL's Los Angeles Kings (the wording has been changed to reflect soccer-specific techniques). The focus is on routines that can be implemented during the flow of play, whether they are preparatory, coping, or refocusing routines.

With the first strategy, players are asked to remind themselves to keep moving, or use "active feet." If players continue to move and stay in tune with the action on the field, important mental effects can occur, including releasing tension and mistakes, increasing energy, and improving anticipation. This point may seem silly, but many players do not breathe correctly. When players get too stressed, anxious, or play "tight," they greatly reduce the amount of oxygen that is being delivered to the system. Whenever breathing becomes short, the body is not maximizing oxygen intake. Players should ensure that they do not allow this situation to occur, especially before a big play

| Routine/Cues | Mental Skill/Action | Mental/Technical Effect |
| --- | --- | --- |
| Active Feet | keep on the move | release tension; present focus; increase energy; refocusing; alleviates watching; improves anticipation |
| Energizing breaths | full breaths | helps to fend off tension & fatigue; energize system |
| Focus within the touchlines | focus on the play on the field | focusing IN on present action not on distractions off-field (stands, bench, scoreboard) |
| 'Park' distractions | refocus; present focus | mistake management; dealing w/distractions, stressors; adversity |
| Refocusing routines: Strategy/Toughness Cues | refocus; present focus; A-B-C's | readiness; confidence enhancement; mistake management |
| Head on a swivel | strategy/toughness cue | increase vision; improved reads & widen attentional focus position; communication; readiness |

Figure 14-4. On-field preparation and refocusing routines

(penalty kick, corner kick, set piece), when they will improve their chance of success if they are totally focused on the moment, aware of their surroundings, and feel energized and ready. Teaching players to "focus between the touchlines" will help them focus on what they have control of and on the job in front of them—the play on the park. Many players are easily distracted by the crowd, the score of the game, or their coaches on the sidelines. If players can keep their focus on the pitch and never beyond the white lines, they will be better able to focus on the moment and not be distracted by what is going on outside of these lines. Since players can only attend to a minimum of cues, they should limit these cues to only what is going on around them on the field of play.

Prior to practice sessions and matches, players should be encouraged to "park" their life stressors and distractions outside of the locker room and playing field. At some schools, the players must walk through a "funnel" prior to walking on the practice field. Before entering the practice field funnel, players must read the practice board, so that they know what drills and exercises they will be doing and what they plan on improving upon during the session. Through the use of this prepractice routine, players focus in on their practice goals by "parking" their stress and assignments outside the practice field's fences.

The use of strategy and toughness cues can be invaluable to players who struggle with letting go of mistakes or in times of adversity (e.g., tough stretch of missed goal chances, missed tackles and headers, fatigue, or nagging injuries). Some players need to refocus after mistakes and prepare for their next touch by devising strategy cues can help them to focus on the present (e.g., the next touch of the ball), and not on the past mistake. Players should not be worrying about what will happen in the future. Strategy cues are similar to technical cues in that the player has a preprogrammed phrase that he uses to help "focus in" on something other than the past mistake or the distractions. These cues could range from goalkeepers saying to themselves, "Get to the angle early and react," midfielders saying, "Support the ball to the target" or "Play the early cross," and defenders saying, "Take up good covering defensive positions." These cues help players to perform their responsibilities more effectively, while also assisting them in moving forward after tough patches of play.

Playing with a "head on a swivel" means viewing as much of the park as possible when needed. When players begin to become too anxious, or put too much pressure on their next touch of the ball, their attentional focus will narrow, thus limiting what they see on the field. What players see in their environment is critical to making quick and effective decisions. When players' attentional focus is too narrow, they will miss valuable cues that can be used to make the best decision on the ball. For example, if midfielders or overlapping defenders fail to see the defensive coverage or their own players' runs away from the ball, they will probably get caught in ball possession and lose the ball. If strikers do not survey the scene prior to ball reception, they are greatly limiting their options when the ball gets played into their feet. Being able to survey the surroundings is critical for most players on the pitch. A players who reminds himself to keep his head on a swivel will continue to survey his surroundings and give himself the best chance at using what he sees to make the most effective decision off the ball or with his next touch. Saying this simple cue will also help the player focus on the present play and not on how nervous he is, on any mistakes he has made, or how "poorly" he is playing.

# Inspirational Toughness

The last barrier to address is a lack of *inspirational toughness.* This component is related to why an athlete plays his sport and what makes the athlete happiest while playing. Athletes play sports for hundreds of reasons. Do you know why your players play soccer? What is each player getting out of the experience? Players' motives for playing are often incongruent with their coaches' motives.

Some coaches believe that all players play to get better and move along to the next level, but unless players are asked what their motives are, and have some of their motives met, they will not be optimally motivated and inspired. Some players play just to be affiliated with a team, others play for the recognition and accolades, and others play for the camaraderie of teammates. Athletes who are not having their primary motives met are less driven to work toward the coach's motives, such as better play, wins, or championships (which are usually the coach's primary motives for coaching), and are thus limited by this inspirational barrier.

> *"The key is spirit. See, the spirit is what gives you the passion on a daily basis."*
> —Hubie Brown, Former Memphis Grizzlies Head Coach
> (*Los Angeles Times*, November 27, 2004)

Asking players what their primary motives are for playing, as well as what their future aspirations are in the game of soccer, will truly help coaches gain access to their players' inner drives and motivations. Once coaches are privy to this information, they have a good button to push when needed. Players will tend to do what is asked of them by the coaches if their personal motives are being met. Players who are not aware of their primary motives are unable to maximize their playing capacities, because inspiration is what drives players to get better in all aspects of their games.

> *"There are still two or three guys who aren't willing to pay the price to win a game. This is not Wal-Mart®. There are no discounts in this league."*
> —Ron Wilson, Head Coach, San Jose Sharks
> (*Los Angeles Times*, October 31, 2003)

Sacrifice, work-ethic, commitment, dedication, risk-taking, and drive are all words that define the inner core of competitiveness. This inner core is what inspires a player and team to do what they do. Players (and teams, for that matter) play out their level of inspiration in their behavior. For example, players and teams that fail to consistently train with quality, continually look for shortcuts, fail in the face of adversity, and are motivated by their individual agendas tend to expose an awful lot about their playing philosophy. Coach Wilson, in the previous quote, made mention of players who are looking for "discounts," or the easy way to success. There are no shortcuts to victory and consistent success. What is not addressed in most coaching education and sport psychology articles and books is the philosophy of players. A player's philosophy guides his practice, work rate, quality (or lack of quality) of training, and commitment to getting better and maximizing potential. This philosophy of playing is synonymous with the level of inspiration.

Players—including youth, collegiate, professional and national team athletes—who are inspired to become the best players they can be have the philosophy and training habits that mirror their drives and goals to be the best. Such players are self-motivated and low-maintenance; they are always there for their coaches and teammates and do what they do on a consistent basis. How many players of this caliber do you have on your team? On the other hand, how many players do you have on your team who are high-maintenance, exhibit lower levels of self-motivation, and whose games go up and down depending upon their attitudes, present levels of play, and whether their personal agendas/motives are being met. So much is said about coaches' philosophies, but what philosophy a player has toward success, optimal performance, the process involved in being a consistent performer, and his training is a large determinant of his lasting success.

*"Leaders need introspection. Knowing yourself—your strengths, your weaknesses, and your values—is essential."*

—Rick Pitino (Janssen & Dale, 2002; p. 55)

Courtesy of USC Sports Information

Figure 14-5. Philosophical coaches are cognizant of how their actions are perceived by their players and seek to empower and inspire them by being good ethical leaders and role models.

The following section discusses the eight aspects of a philosophical athlete. These characteristics could and should be applied to coaches as well. Both players and coaches can make the most out of their athletic experiences by learning as much as they can about themselves and how sport plays a role in their lives, as opposed to simply learning about the technical/tactical aspects of the game. When players can internalize the lessons learned from their sporting experience and apply them to their lives, they tend to embrace the challenge and processes involved in the mastery of skills in the competitive arena. Players who appreciate the process of competing, rather than simply the outcome, give themselves the best chance of steering clear of performance barriers and strive to play better than they did previously. How *philosophical* are you as a coach? How *philosophical* are your players?

*Philosophical players value the sport experience as an opportunity to learn about themselves.* They take their sporting experience seriously, yet appreciate it as a game and value it as such. They also take advantage of the many lessons that can be learned through sport, such as winning, losing, dealing with adversity and setbacks, team unity, and leadership.

*Philosophical players take responsibility for actions, attitudes, and the pursuit of meaningful goals.* Soccer is a team game that allows for plenty of opportunities to practice "social loafing," whereby players let someone else do the dirty work and give more to the team effort. Consider those teammates who do not track back to offer good covering positions on defense. They are shirking their defensive responsibilities, because they are tired, want to "save" themselves for the latter moments of the game, or are "cheating" on defense so that they are in an advanced position on the attack. When goals are given up, or games are lost, philosophical players do not look for someone to blame. They look at themselves first, and then seek to learn lessons to assure that history does not repeat itself.

*Philosophical players show respect for themselves, teammates, coaches, family members, the opponent, and the ideals of the sport.* Respectful players play within the rules of the game and steer clear from playing "on the fringe" through bad gamesmanship practices (trash-talking, tugging of jerseys, clipping ankles, and other "shady" practices). In this fashion, they are also showing respect for their opponents by not attempting to "tilt" the level playing field in their favor by "bending" the rules or cheating. Respectful players want to challenge themselves and their teammates by beating the opponents on a level playing field—may the best team win. Respectful players also respect their coaches and teammates by following team rules and adequately preparing for practice and game play by living a balanced life, taking care of their school work, and not getting into trouble outside of the pitch.

*Philosophical players accept their identity through sport, without overly identifying with the sport experience.* Mentally tough players are able to deal effectively with adversity, such as poor play, reduced playing time, or minor or major injuries, because they are able to stay confident and process-focused. They take on the persona and attitude that it is "going to take more than this (adversity) to keep me down." So many players are ruined in the face of adversity because so much is tied to their sporting experience. Who they are and how they are perceived and viewed by the world is tied to the fact that they are soccer players. This type of thinking only works to limit them as players and as people.

This situation is especially evident in the wake of an injury. The player views this situation as going from being an important contributor to the team's efforts to being an "outsider" who is no longer as important. This type of attitude is debilitative for coping, rehabilitating, strengthening, and enhancing speed of recovery, and could have adverse effects on the team if the player does not adjust productively to the injury. Players who are able to work through the adverse situation (e.g., injury), and stay connected and continue to contribute in any way possible, will aid themselves and their team in moving forward. Having a keen awareness of how much of a player's identity is tied to soccer is important, because balance is essential. A player must know that he is more than just an attacking midfielder, for example. This knowledge will better prepare him for adversity, as well as make him a happier player and person.

*Philosophical players embrace their moments of challenge, which are also referred to as self-revealing moments.* Throughout the sporting experience, players are often faced with moments of extreme challenge. Examples include keepers who are facing a breakaway in the closing seconds of a match while up a goal; the player who takes the fifth penalty kick in a must-score situation; and an athlete playing his first minutes on the varsity field. How do players fare when put in situations such as these? How players perceive these moments (fight or flight), welcome (or not) these challenges, and how they deal with the outcome (take responsibility or blame) tells an awful lot about the playing philosophy of the player. Philosophical players plan, prepare, and embrace these defining moments. Regardless of the ultimate outcome, players take what they can from these experiences and learn how best to manage the situation the next time it occurs. The most important lesson they can take from these self-revealing moments is how they handled themselves and what they learned about themselves throughout the process. Coaches who reinforce the processes undertaken by players (attitude, work rate, confidence, ethics, team play) can truly empower players to gain a greater appreciation for what they have accomplished and the path it required to do so.

*Philosophical players seek "lived knowledge" in their sporting endeavors by appreciating not only what is learned during play, but also the experience of being a soccer player.* Much is written about the "zone," "runner's high," or "peak experience" in sport. Phil Jackson, coach of the Los Angeles Lakers, in his book *Sacred Hoops,* talked extensively about his peak experiences as a player and coach. Although seemingly mystical in its interpretations, any person and player can experience a peak experience, whether they are driving, playing a sport, or working in some capacity. The peak experience is ripe for sportsmen, since players are exposed to ever-changing situations and challenges. Coaches are in an ideal position to have an open dialogue with their players about peak experience in sports. Getting into a discussion about each player's best experiences on the field can be an interesting and empowering experience. Learning what each player did, felt, and experienced prior to, during, and after moments in the "zone" can be a valuable learning experience. It can also engage the team in talking about something other than wins and losses, such as a true appreciation of the game, and help players embrace their respective motives for playing the great game of soccer (inspirational capacity).

*Philosophical players adopt a process orientation, where they set out to outcompete themselves on a daily basis, rather than simply beating someone else.* Imagine what a difficult task it was for Michael Jordan to outdo himself every game. Some players are driven more by an outcome orientation, with which they set out just to get the win, regardless of what it takes to get there. Adopting this type of philosophy opens up the possibility of unethical practices, since the "ends justify the means." Players who are all about just getting the wins will utilize gamesmanship and unsportsmanlike behaviors and actions to improve their chances of succeeding. Practices such as taking performance-enhancing drugs, bending the rules as far as possible, and doing what is necessary to tip the scale in their favor should not be held in high esteem. Wins that come from these practices are tainted and should not be valued nearly as much as those wins that come from pure competition—if they are valued at all. Philosophical players want their opponents to bring their best to the pitch, because it will bring out the best in them. This situation is the only way to determine who the better team was on any given day.

Coaches may try to sell this approach and philosophy to their players, but what they say and do may run counter to this philosophy. Empowering players with a process-oriented philosophy will help the coach in more ways than one. Players will maintain a high level of confidence, because they will continue to gauge their improvements from game to game, instead of getting bogged down by the wins and losses. Players must realize that winning is still important, but the means of getting the win is where the emphasis should be placed. The team should adhere to the team vision and set standards even if they have lost a few matches. Teams that set goals such as "being undefeated" and "winning a national championship" will be empowered and motivated until they lose. Putting the focus on the everyday training, and improving as an individual and team on a daily and game-to-game basis, will greatly improve the chances of getting "Ws."

Remember, winning matches is something of an "uncontrollable." One team may be the most talented, have the most physically gifted players, and boast the best coaches in the league, but they can give up a goal to a counterattack against the run of play and lose 1-0. All that players and teams can control is their preparation, work rate, mental toughness, and quality execution—the outcome will take care of itself. Players, teams, and coaches who do not learn this lesson are playing a "fool's game." Everyone who competes at a high level—collegiate players, national team members, Olympic athletes, and professional athletes—wants to win, needs to win (to stay employed in most cases), and so enjoys the adulation and feelings of obtaining the win. But what must be stressed is the *process* of getting the win. If coaches, players, and teams can improve their play from game to game, the wins will come. Forcing the win will only trigger the voluminous performance barriers already addressed in this book. Basketball Zen master Phil Jackson once remarked that it is important not to force the action, but instead allow it to naturally unfold. This technique takes patience, confidence, and a lot of trust—three important intangibles that tend to make up a philosophical athlete.

*Philosophical players are keenly aware of when and why they utilize self-handicapping statements and actions.* Once aware, they combat the need to use these statements and actions and instead focus on what is in their control, such as their preparatory routines and rehearsal of what they need to do to best help the squad. Self-handicapping is a strategy used by players to protect their ego, self-esteem, and standing on the team in case they play poorly. Examples of self-handicapping strategies include making excuses prior to playing, embellishing an actual event that is deemed to impede play, or sabotaging themselves or their equipment prior to or during play.

The most common self-handicapping strategy is pregame excuse making. A player who utilizes this strategy gives an excuse to his teammates, parents, coaches, or whoever else will listen—maybe that he is not feeling well or is still recovering from an injury—so that if he has a subpar night on the pitch, not only can the player refer back to the excuse, but the observers will also attribute the poor play to the excuse. In this way, the player protects himself from internal questioning, but also controls what the "audience" will perceive of his play. The use of self-handicapping strategies is fueled by the fear of being "found out." An athlete who does not have a solid base of self-esteem and playing confidence fears that he will be discovered as a bad player. Out of this fear, the player will do whatever is necessary to protect this discovery from taking place.

Another strategy that players use is to embellish stories or events to attempt to derive sympathy or compassion from observers, to again lay the foundation (of excuses) in case play is not to a high standard. These excuses have a little Hollywood drama inserted for full effect. Many coaches have heard tales of sleepless nights, food poisoning, fire alarms in the dorms, all-night study sessions, flat tires and car trouble, extreme sickness, acts of heroism, and so on. Real events can always happen and should be handled with all seriousness, but these players take minor incidents and blow them up to be a lot bigger than they are.

Self-sabotage includes the player altering his equipment, pregame routine, or even hurting himself just enough to have a built-in excuse. Incidents may include playing with only one contact lens (saying the other one popped out), playing in old boots ("one of these days I have to buy new ones"), playing in boots that are too big or too small, or keepers using old gloves (no gripping). Sometimes these actions are done without the player really putting too much stock in them, but they still do them. Procrastination is often a way of not dealing with a need that should be met, but instead the player keeps putting it off in an effort to escape from doing something about it. Players who utilize self-handicapping often know what they are doing and why they are doing it. They unfortunately procrastinate doing anything about it. Other examples include altering the pregame ritual, especially if these players are superstitious and know that their teammates know these rituals. "Losing" a lucky head band is one way to build an excuse for himself. Not giving themselves enough time to warm-up and stretch is another strategy that players use to lay the foundation of excuses. Players and coaches should be cognizant of these types of actions and intervene accordingly.

Excuse building is like telling one little white lie—the first one works and gets you off the hook, so you do it again, and again, and again. Self-handicapping is a defense mechanism that does not help players learn to play and live to the fullest. These players are not risk takers, and they like to be able to play and not have to worry about negative comments being hurled their way. They want to play "protected" and "save face." They hardly ever put in an all-out effort on the field, because if they do, and they fail, they will surely be discovered as being bad players. Fear of failure drives this type of irrational thinking. The strategies outlined in Chapters 12 and 13 can help these fearful players transform themselves into fearless players.

Philosophical athletes, or "fearless" players, do not play these "mind games," because they have a sound sense of self-esteem and playing confidence, and they embrace the challenges that come with competitive sport. The last thing they want to do is to give the opponent an advantage over them. How well can a player perform with defective equipment or impaired vision? Fearless competitors embrace the uncertainty, the ever-changing environment, and the knowledge that anyone can win soccer matches. These athletes are risk-takers because they are willing to play all-out without the fears experienced by so many athletes. The more coaches learn about each of their players, and are cognizant of any pregame banter and excuse making, the better position they will be in to step in and transform these fearful players into fearless, philosophical competitors.

# Chapter Summary

- Players who are more aware of their thoughts and self-talk, and develop plans for dealing with inappropriate and damaging thoughts and self-talk, are more consistent performers and perform better in pressure situations.

- When most players think about negative things and get down on themselves, they usually play their worst soccer.

- Confident athletes believe that they can and will play well every time out on the field. Players who are able to think this way do not let their play dictate their confidence. Rather, their confidence level remains high, thus dictating their performance.

- Taking advantage of the many sources of performance confidence can be a tremendous way to optimize player confidence and performance.

- Gaining control and mastery over intensity is one of the most important things players (and coaches) can do to improve practice and game readiness.

- Being overintense is not the only way that intensity can impede players' progress. Being underintense has its own causes and brings its own performance consequences.

- To be effective at "freeing the mind," players must be able to foster adequate attention and concentration control. Doing so requires the ability to focus and switch attention as needed during pressure situations.

- One of the major ways in which distractions affect performance is by consuming limited attentional capacities. Attending to these distractions evokes psychological, physiological, or emotional reactions that can take many players off their top games.

- One of the more important factors contributing to top performances is the ability to generate and maintain optimal readiness prior to execution.

- For players to maximize their capacities for consistent, optimal play in practice and matches, they must be inspired to play. Inspirational barriers can be costly to the athlete by sapping the love and passion for the game.

- Philosophical players are more ethical, confident, resilient, fearless, and mentally tough, because they are respectful, learn about themselves through sport, are balanced in sport and life, practice productive thinking, and are process-focused.

# Section IV:
# Training and Coaching Effectiveness

# 15

# Quality of Practice: Coach and Player Responsibilities

Although automaticity may come a little more easily and quickly to players who have loads of natural talent, all players need to work to improve upon their skills and mechanics by putting in their reps. A universal goal for coaches of all sports is to maximize the efficiency of practice time. Practice is where it all gets done—physical training, technical work, implementation of systems, training of the mental game, and simulation of game conditions—so that players are totally prepared for match play.

The quality of an individual athlete's practices is considered to be one of the most critical determinants of optimal performance. Unfortunately for coaches and athletes, a paucity of material has been available that addresses how to maximize practice opportunities. Thus, the purpose of this section is to address this topic from an integrated approach that links the responsibilities of both players and coaches to improve upon the quality of individual and team training.

Utilizing the theoretical, empirical, and practical work from numerous disciplines (e.g., motor learning, pedagogy, and applied sport psychology), four major factors have been developed that encapsulate the most important areas that both athletes and coaches should address in an effort to improve the quality of training of the individual and team—attitude, preparation, execution, and evaluation. Specifically, these four main factors are discussed in detail, ranging from coach and player *attitudes* toward training and specific *preparation* practices, to *execution* strategies and *evaluating* a player's performance after training.

> *"I approach practices the same way I approach games... You can't turn it on and off like a faucet. I can't dog it during practice and then, when I need that extra push late in the game, expect it to be there."*
> —Michael Jordan (Williams, 1997, p. 197)

# Quality of Training—Athletes' Responsibilities

> *"Players must accept the link between training and competition and be willing to train at an intensity that will make transfer possible. It is foolish to train at 60 percent intensity and hope that it will transfer to 100 percent on game day—how you practice is how you play!"*
> —Bill Beswick, Mental Skills Trainer for English Premier Club
> Derby County (2001, p. 55)

## Quality Attitude

For athletes to train to the upper range of their potential, it is critical that they take responsibility at the onset for improving upon the quality of their training by adopting a quality attitude. Pete Carroll, head football coach at repeat national champion USC, spoke at a conference and stated that an important distinction exists between players who have a professional attitude and those with a mediocre attitude. The major difference between these two attitudes is how players perceive practice. Some players view practice as an opportunity to play and improve, which denotes an internally driven motivation mainly within the player's control. Others, however, perceive practice as something that is "done to them," signifying an externally driven motivation that is out of a player's control (Voight, 2002).

If a player has a mediocre attitude, his effort in practice will fluctuate depending upon mood, whether or not he likes the activity, or on external motivation. Players with this mindset go through the motions, put in their time, and just want to complete the drill and get off the field. Players with a professional attitude, on the other hand, view practice as an opportunity for improvement and refinement, not something "forced" onto them. Such athletes ask the following questions: How can I/we get better today? What will I/we accomplish today? Athletes set standards of performance for each practice and each week of practice, and evaluate their practice performance in terms of execution, effort, and overall quality, while also seeking feedback regarding their practice performance.

Figure 15-1. Professional-attitude players view practice as an opportunity to improve technical execution.

Professional-attitude athletes take more responsibility for their performances by holding themselves accountable to preset standards of execution. Another important aspect of an athlete's attitude is his "coachability," which can be defined by the player's willingness to put in near maximal effort on drill work and practice/competition, listen to coaching points and attempt to implement them into action, and accept feedback of all types (corrective, positive, punitive, encouragement). In most cases, a player's level of coachability can be altered, especially in the case of "uncoachable" players, although this change takes work from all parties (coach, athletes, parents, friends, teammates) and a special coach to undo some of the wrongs, which may have led to the present uncoachable condition.

Closely tied to coachability is the motivation and work rate of the players. Professional-attitude athletes tend to be motivated by internal desires to improve and perform better than they did in their last performance, thus increasing their motivation and work rate to do all they can in practice to ensure that this improvement occurs. Conversely, mediocre-attitude athletes tend to be motivated by external agents (praise, big game, crowd, accolades, media), yet in the absence of these agents—as in the case in practice—motivation is lacking. These mediocre-attitude athletes usually consider themselves "gamers" and do not feel that it is important to give a near-maximal effort in training. These players can also be considered "part-time" players because they only really play at game time. These "gamers" believe that they can just turn on their top performances like a light without having to put in the work in practice. Although these players may be quite talented and succeed come game time, their consistency of play will not be as sharp and their long-term progress may be jeopardized by the lack of consistent, quality practice.

## Quality Preparation

How many players actually prepare for practice? Most players probably shove down a burger, race to the locker room, busily put on their gear, get to the practice field, and wait until they are told what to do. Sounds like a mediocre-attitude athlete. A professional-attitude athlete will attempt to find a way to prepare better for practice. Actually having a set routine to follow, made up of proper eating (fueling up) and rest, as well as finding a way to let go of non-soccer-related problems (school, friends, significant others) can ensure that the two hours of practice can be dedicated solely to quality execution. The ability to park distractions is an important skill to acquire. It is very difficult to truly commit and focus on practice if outside stressors are brought onto the field. One routine that has worked with several top players is to write down the stressors that are nagging them, and, prior to walking onto the field, shredding or throwing this paper away, symbolically throwing away the stressors so that the player can focus on practice objectives.

> *"Athletes…know that a gap often exists between their knowledge and their behavior. There are those who usually do what is necessary; others often do what is necessary; some rarely do. Those who never do what is necessary are not around long enough to be otherwise convinced. Preparation is the key."*
> —Harv Dorfman, Author, Mental-Skills Trainer for Major League Baseball (2003, p. 309)

Coaches can be a great help in assisting athletes with their practice preparation by setting up prepractice routines, such as arriving to the field prior to the start of practice to perform a wide array of warm-up activities. Players who do this routine can be truly ready to begin practice once the coaches arrive. Also, athletes can prepare better for practice by setting standards of performance (goals) for each week's practice or individual session (e.g., "What do I want to accomplish by the first preseason scrimmage? What do I want to accomplish in this defending drill?"). In addition to setting standards, players can *visualize* what they want to accomplish prior to physically and technically executing the drill. Another strategy that top players have used is to mentally picture themselves executing their most important roles and responsibilities over and over again, often the night before practice or prior to practice. Strikers would shoot 100 shots a night before bedtime in their mind's eye. Keepers would make crossed-ball saves and block a certain amount of shots. Each position could easily do this type of "homework" every day or night. Visualizing these actions help to devise a mental blueprint that is used during real, physical training. The more often players perform their particular actions, both in their heads and with a real ball, the more reps they are putting in.

## Quality Execution

Mediocre-attitude athletes often go through the motions and do just enough during practice so they do not get yelled at or called out. Professional-attitude athletes have set purposes and objectives for each practice session and view practice as a valuable opportunity. They also utilize techniques geared toward their own quality execution, whereas the "mediocres" attempt to survive the session. It is important that coaches not just let practice end; instead, coaches should make sure that players finish practice. Examples of quality execution techniques used by professional-attitude athletes include the following:

- Taking notes during a team meeting, or after practice sessions, regarding specific points they find important, especially coaching points on technical and tactical elements.
- Evaluating practice performance "on the fly" or during practice, so they can be more aware of what is working versus what is not. "Mediocres" just want to get to the end of practice and are not aware of how they are doing.
- Devising competitions with themselves to increase the quality of execution. For example, if a professional-attitude athlete is doing sprint work, he attempts to chase down a teammate instead of just trying to survive the running. During technical work, a professional-attitude athlete counts the number of successful attempts made instead of just doing the drill until the coach stops it (again, merely surviving).
- Utilizing preset routines when concentration begins to drift during practice. Professional-attitude athletes utilize refocusing routines to ensure that when focus fades they have a routine from which to draw.
- Knowing exactly why they are doing a certain drill, what the end result should look like, and what they should be focusing on during execution. This knowledge can have a big impact on the quality of effort and execution. These issues should be discussed prior to drill execution. Although this responsibility primarily lies with the coaches, players should ask if they do know the answer to these pertinent questions.

## Quality Control

Once practice is done, do players evaluate their performance? Professional-attitude players ask themselves the following questions:

- How was my physical, technical, and tactical execution?
- How was my work rate?
- What were the strengths and weaknesses of my play?
- What will I do differently during my next practice?
- What should I do in preparation for the next practice?
- What helped to motivate me for practice today?
- How did I refocus and stay focused today?
- What did the coaches say to me regarding my practice performance?

Mediocre-attitude players do not ask these questions. They are simply pleased that practice is over.

Using standards and goals is very helpful, especially if a coach has players who evaluate their progress. If players accomplish a particular goal, they should take pride in their accomplishment and press on with higher goals. If goals are not accomplished, players should then reevaluate their performance (positives/negatives), and either start fresh to accomplish the goal the next day or revise the goal.

A survey has been developed to assess the use of the essential quality practice techniques by top players in their respective sports (Figure 15-2). Obtaining this feedback can be an excellent springboard for discussion with individual players and the team. Players should be informed of the results, with the trust that they will only be used to assist the athletes in their play and not as a punishment in any way. For example, no player should be called out for having low scores on the subscales. Players will derive the appropriate feedback if they score it themselves as well, but this survey will be more valuable if the coach is active in the process. As with any questionnaire, players can record answers that they know the coach wants to see, but this practice can be limited if the coach explains the importance of honest responses, and that the results will only be used to better each player's training habits.

# Quality of Training —Coaches' Responsibilities

## Quality Attitude

Coaches should do all they can to be aware of their specific coaching philosophy and behaviors, as well as the effects that these attitudes and behaviors have on their athletes. As the leadership literature indicates, athletes have numerous preferences for specific coaching behaviors. If athletes feel that they are not getting the adequate amount of a preferred coaching behavior, their level of satisfaction and performance could be hindered. The effect of this discrepancy between preferred and perceived behaviors could be further exacerbated by a lack of awareness on the part of the coach. Coaches who are more aware of their own attitudes and behaviors, and how their

## Training Survey

Please read each statement and fill in the most appropriate word by circling the corresponding number from 0 to 5 (never to always). *Note*: Your responses should refer to your usual training habits.

**KEY:**

| Never: 0 | Rarely: 1 | Sometimes: 2 | Often: 3 | Very often: 4 | Always: 5 |
|---|---|---|---|---|---|

| | | | | | |
|---|---|---|---|---|---|
| 1.) I _____ look forward to practice. | 0 | 1 | 2 | 3 | 4 | 5 |
| 2.) I _____ "go through the motions" in practices. | 0 | 1 | 2 | 3 | 4 | 5 |
| 3.) I _____ consider practice to be an opportunity to improve. | 0 | 1 | 2 | 3 | 4 | 5 |
| 4.) Before practice, I _____ have in mind what I am going to try to improve. | 0 | 1 | 2 | 3 | 4 | 5 |
| 5.) I _____ feel that practice is something that coach "does to us." | 0 | 1 | 2 | 3 | 4 | 5 |
| 6.) I _____ look forward to the end of practice. | 0 | 1 | 2 | 3 | 4 | 5 |
| 7.) I _____ start thinking about practice well before it starts. | 0 | 1 | 2 | 3 | 4 | 5 |
| 8.) If I feel tired or do not like the drills, I _____ have a good practice. | 0 | 1 | 2 | 3 | 4 | 5 |
| 9.) I _____ use a routine to help get me "ready" for practice. | 0 | 1 | 2 | 3 | 4 | 5 |
| 10.) I _____ fuel up prior to practice by eating the right food and hydrating myself. | 0 | 1 | 2 | 3 | 4 | 5 |
| 11.) I _____ find out from the coaching staff what type of things we will do in practice for the week/upcoming session. | 0 | 1 | 2 | 3 | 4 | 5 |
| 12.) If available, I _____ review video tape of practices/games to target my goals for practices. | 0 | 1 | 2 | 3 | 4 | 5 |
| 13.) I _____ ask for coaches' feedback to help target my practice goals. | 0 | 1 | 2 | 3 | 4 | 5 |
| 14.) I _____ do mental and physical preparation prior to practice. | 0 | 1 | 2 | 3 | 4 | 5 |
| 15.) I am _____ able to leave non-sport issues (classwork, family) and distractions outside of the practice field. | 0 | 1 | 2 | 3 | 4 | 5 |
| 16.) I _____ do relaxation or "psych-up" techniques prior to practice if I feel I need it to get ready & motivated. | 0 | 1 | 2 | 3 | 4 | 5 |
| 17.) I _____ take notes during team meetings and video sessions. | 0 | 1 | 2 | 3 | 4 | 5 |
| 18.) During practice, I _____ evaluate my play in terms of what is working, what isn't, and areas I can improve. | 0 | 1 | 2 | 3 | 4 | 5 |
| 19.) I _____ put in maximal effort when I practice. | 0 | 1 | 2 | 3 | 4 | 5 |
| 20.) I _____ use a refocusing routine when I find myself "drifting" during practice. | 0 | 1 | 2 | 3 | 4 | 5 |
| 21.) During conditioning/fitness work, I _____ challenge myself by passing a teammate, or beating my last time. | 0 | 1 | 2 | 3 | 4 | 5 |
| 22.) I _____ try and help my teammates improve their work rate in practice via vocal encouragement and by my example. | 0 | 1 | 2 | 3 | 4 | 5 |

Figure 15-2. Quality-of-training survey for players

| | | | | | | |
|---|---|---|---|---|---|---|
| 23.) During drill work, I _____ use "challenging Games," like counting the number of successful reps, to improve my practice performance. | 0 | 1 | 2 | 3 | 4 | 5 |
| 24.) I am _____ receptive to feedback regarding my play from teammates and coaches. | 0 | 1 | 2 | 3 | 4 | 5 |
| 25.) After practice, I _____ evaluate what I did well, in addition to what I did not do well. | 0 | 1 | 2 | 3 | 4 | 5 |
| 26.) After practice, I _____ ask my coaches for feedback regarding my practice performance. | 0 | 1 | 2 | 3 | 4 | 5 |
| 27.) I _____ think about practice once it is over. | 0 | 1 | 2 | 3 | 4 | 5 |
| 28.) After practice I _____ plan what I will work on for the next training session. | 0 | 1 | 2 | 3 | 4 | 5 |
| 29.) If I feel I need added work in a particular part of my play, I will _____ spend extra time on it after practice. | 0 | 1 | 2 | 3 | 4 | 5 |
| 30.) I _____ evaluate my mental game (strengths and weaknesses) upon completion of practice. | 0 | 1 | 2 | 3 | 4 | 5 |
| 31.) I _____ think about how I can improve the mental aspects of my play. | 0 | 1 | 2 | 3 | 4 | 5 |
| 32.) After practice, I _____ provide feedback to the coaches regarding the practice session (what I liked, what worked, what we need to do more of next time). | 0 | 1 | 2 | 3 | 4 | 5 |

Scoring Procedures:

✓ High scores represent excellent training attitudes and habits
✓ Reverse score items 2, 5, and 6 (0=5; 1=4; 2=3; 3=2; 4=1; 5=0)
✓ Four Subscales: Scores range from 0–40

     Subscale 1: Questions 1–8 = Quality Attitude
     Subscale 2: Questions 9–16 = Quality Preparation
     Subscale 3: Questions 17–24 = Quality Execution
     Subscale 4: Questions 25–32 = Quality Control

✓ Subscale score ranges:

    *33–40    Wish the team were full of these "trainers"! You are fully maximizing your capacities.
    *25–32    Very good training habits! Always do what is necessary.
    *17–24    Good training habits overall—some areas are in need of attention; often do what is necessary.
    *9–16    Poor training habits—some real work is necessary to improve; rarely do what is necessary.
    *0–8    Bad training habits—will catch up with you someday; never do what is necessary.

✓ Quality Attitude =         _____
✓ Quality Preparation =     _____
✓ Quality Execution =       _____
✓ Quality Control =          _____

players perceive them, may have players who are more satisfied and perform better. It has been written that the quality of an athlete's sport experience reflects the beliefs and attitudes of the coach.

*"To be a good coach, you need to recognize the effect you have in everything you do with your team, say to your team, [and how you] behave around your team."*
—Pete Waite, Head Volleyball Coach, Wisconsin (2002, p. 304)

Courtesy of USC Sports Information

Figure 15-3. To be most effective, coaches must be aware of how their feedback and actions are perceived by their players—miscommunication can lead to many barriers to optimal performance.

Another critical aspect of a coach's attitude is his openness to the mental aspects of sport. Although many coaches cite mental factors for the team's and players' successes and failures, how many of these coaches actually train the mental side of their sport? As mentioned in Chapter 11, it is important for coaches to know that incorporating mental-skills training into everyday coaching can enhance coaching effectiveness, as well as players' quality of practice play, both of which can transfer onto the game field.

Many coaches, however, do put a priority on improving upon all aspects of their players' performance, especially the mental side. For example, some coaches help establish set routines whereby the players begin to prepare for practice before the opening whistle. Bruce Synder, former head football coach at Arizona State University, created a set of routines so that players could leave their school, family, friends, and other college issues/concerns in their cars or their rooms (referred to as "parking"), and not take them into the locker room. Thus, once they enter the locker room they were football players, and their entire focus was on this endeavor.

Figure 15-4. What separates soccer from other games is that soccer is played on the field with little control over the action by coaches, which definitely makes for some tense times for coaches. For this reason, enhancing upon the quality of training sessions is tantamount for a successful season.

## Quality Preparation

The first strategy that can be used to enhance preparation is helping players devise individual standards and goals for the upcoming practices. Players who are informed about the objectives, the standards to which they will be held, and the ways in which they can meet the standards and accomplish the goals, will have a more motivated, productive attitude. Thus, these athletes may be better prepared for the practice session than those players who go into practice uninformed. Players who are uninformed and are not given explicit directions and standards are more likely to simply go through the motions if left to their own devices. Additionally, using different modalities (e.g., learning styles) to communicate these important messages, such as verbal communication, graphic displays, and physical demonstrations, has been shown to be an effective pedagogical strategy.

A second method used to improve preparation is to teach players how to improve focus, as well as ways to reestablish focus when facing adversity. First, coaches can set up prepractice routines for players, with the goal of helping them park stressors and distractions outside of the playing field. Some coaches have established a "concentration line," or a funnel that players must walk across or through prior to entering practice so that they can focus on training rather than on all their nonsoccer issues and problems (see Figure 14-5). Additionally, players who lose focus during practice should have preset refocusing routines handy. The University of Nebraska Football coaches, with the help of mental trainer Ken Ravizza (Osbourne & Ravizza, 1988), formulated a routine that helped to instill a sense of "refocus" once the players began to drift, thus, causing a breakdown in play execution. This routine was called the three R's, *Ready-Respond-Refocus*. It was so useful that they began to use it during games when the quarterback needed his teammates to listen to the play call in the huddle. Such a routine could be applied on the field, especially after conceding goals. A similar routine is used at USC. After conceding goals the team gets in a huddle and the keeper and captains say a few cues that help the team refocus and move past the moment. Other examples of preparation and execution routines are listed in Chapter 14. With the use of standards and refocusing routines, players' preparation for practice may greatly be enhanced, thereby improving upon quality execution.

Another important area for self-examination for coaches is to critique the structure of practice sessions. According to the motor learning research literature, learning is enhanced if the practice environment is structured according to the following principles of practice: teaching progressions, practice variability, and game simulation.

*"The coaches who are the best motivators know how to keep their athletes interested and involved. This happens during practices."*
—Harv Dorfman, Author, Mental-Skills Trainer for
Major League Baseball (2003, p. 168)

Players who are being taught either new skills or new "wrinkles" to old skills should be brought through deliberate skill progressions, ranging from simple to complex. What makes the progressions complex is the variability of practice, which includes predesigned conditions that increase visual and auditory distractions so that the skill is performed under changing conditions. These visual and auditory distractions, also referred to as contextual interference elements, can range from changing the speed and timing with which the particular skill pattern is executed and performing the skill under the pressure of opposition or space, to practicing specific game conditions (e.g., scrimmaging with the score of 1-1, or being down or up late in the game). Coaches cannot expect their players to execute in pressure situations if they do not practice these situations during practice time. Ken Ravizza, former mental trainer for several professional baseball teams, advises coaches to practice halftime talks and time-outs. This work is done so that players will practice listening and applying what was said on the game court during pressure situations. Thus, it is very important to simulate game conditions in practice sessions by increasing the use of contextual interference variables.

Coaches who are cognizant of the ways in which teaching progressions, practice variability, and contextual interference can affect players' practices, are in better positions to continue to increase the learning and performing of their athletes. Taking the time needed to address these concerns while preparing for practice sessions seems warranted.

## Quality Execution

As previously stated, simulating game situations in practice is critical for enhancing the players' execution during match play. Immersing players in all that will occur during an actual game prepares them for what they will experience later, including the speed of play, potential distractions, and pressure situations. Anson Dorrance, head women's soccer coach at North Carolina, not only simulates game play, but he and his staff also chart competitions between players. For example, they chart fitness tests, one-on-one duels, small team matches, and technical skill checks to enhance competitiveness by pitting teammate against teammate. His players have repeatedly stated that match play is actually easier than their practice sessions (Dorrance, 1996).

Courtesy of Tennessee Chattanooga Sports Information

Figure 15-5. Coaches should take full advantage of "teachable moments."

Another way to improve execution is through the advantageous use of "teachable moments." Research has indicated that the appropriate use of feedback is a critical determinant to learning. Teachable moments are those prime opportunities that coaches use to teach, instruct, direct, encourage, praise, and punish. Spotting these moments is one of the challenges, the other being what to do with these teachable moments. Being able to differentiate between very good, good, and poor technical execution takes time, experience, and expertise. A player doing a technical and tactical element correctly is having an ideal teachable moment, because the moment acts as a model—a picture of how it should be done. Although corrective feedback is important, all players like to hear when they are doing something well. The challenge for them and their teammates is to repeat this positive, productive action.

The following strategies can help in analyzing skill execution (Fischman & Oxendine, 1998):

- Make several observations to compare players' patterns of execution with correct technique. Taking only a quick look can bias the needs analysis.
- Select one error at a time, and identify the most critical error first, specifying the particular part of the skill that went wrong.
- Determine the cause of the error and specify what the athlete must do to correct it. Keep in mind that hasty error correction may not lead to an increase in performance, because it could cause the athlete to doubt the ability and knowledge of his coaches.
- Stop the action to offer praise and encouragement (catch players doing things correctly) if it is deserved. The critical word in the previous sentence is "deserved." If coaches go too far and offer too much praise, especially if an action was fundamental and not praiseworthy, the coach will lose credibility and the players will then perceive that a lower standard is being accepted.

In addition, feedback may be provided to motivate and energize, not just to provide critical performance information, such as error correction, knowledge of results and performance, specific teaching cues, reinforcement, and punishment. The less frequent the feedback, the more empowering it becomes. Too much feedback may become distracting to the players, and cause them to think too much about their performance (paralysis by overanalysis). Finally, feedback should be provided during skill execution (concurrent) or at the conclusion of the skill pattern (terminal). A good mix of both is recommended.

Two notable coaches have commented on the importance of the types and content of feedback used with their elite players and teams. Tony Dicicco, former coach of the Women's World Cup championship soccer team, has been noted for stressing the importance of these teachable moments by catching players doing things right and not always waiting for a mistake to occur to offer feedback. Pete Carroll, head football coach at USC, noted that the timing and content of feedback are critical to improving subsequent performance. He believes that the sooner the correction is made the better, and if the players are corrected negatively, they will only remember the negative. Thus, if the corrective feedback is consistently negative, the real message is not getting across to the athletes, and subsequent learning and change will seldom occur, thus wasting the teachable moment. Providing negative messages not only confuses players, but it also serves to de-motivate and un-inspire. If coaches have to yell at players during matches, then they have not properly taught the players during practice all week. Harvey Dorfman, a mental-skills trainer, stressed the importance of using "real language," or, as he stated, "mapping out the real territory in real language" (2003, p. 50).

- Be specific, not vague.
- Know the difference between verifiable feedback and feedback that is based on opinion and judgments.
- When comparisons are used, ensure that they are accurate and to the point.
- Be concise when instructing—players want to play and not sit and listen to speeches.
- Watch the use of "emotional" words, such as "he's a wimp."
- Avoid generalizations—to make a point stick, the coach needs to be able to verify what he says.
- Make distinctions "between fact (the final score), inference (we lost because you didn't come to play), and value judgment (the officials were out to get us)"

> *"If you yell at them after every mistake, you will stifle their growth. They will become tentative when they need to be aggressive, and their minds will get in the way of their progress."*
> —Pete Waite, Head Volleyball Coach, Wisconsin (2002, p. 304)

Other methods of improving team execution are to use creative scoring methods and to alternate starters and reserve players during game scrimmages. First, through the use of creative scoring methods, coaches can emphasize what they want players to work on within game-simulated drills and scrimmages. The teams may continue to play from even, up, and down scores to work on their "finishing" ability (defending leads), as well as their ability to come back when down or tied. Also, the better players should sometimes play on the second team, and the reserve players should sometimes play with the first team during team scrimmages. USC's head football coach, Pete Carroll, has used this technique for many years. "One thing Pete does is take the starting quarterback and give him a bunch of reps with the B squad, which helps liven that squad up. The B offense works a lot harder because they know they have the starter taking snaps behind them. And the quarterback knows he has to step up his play to win with that particular squad" (Anderson, 2003, p. 21). Moves such as these increase the capability of both sides, thereby improving the overall team.

A final point to improving the quality of execution is to utilize different teaching modalities to appeal to every player's most salient learning style. Such styles include visual (e.g., walk-throughs, shadow training, use of video and chalk-talks), auditory (e.g., verbal instruction, lectures), kinesthetic (e.g., focus on how the action or movement feels), and imagery (e.g., visualize the tactical strategy or technique prior to actually acting it out). The coach should utilize different teaching modalities, as well as provide for adequate repetition of the desired technical skills to bring about optimal learning and the transfer of skill from one drill to the next. Continuous repetitions, referred to as overlearning, is an important contributor to optimal learning and should be practiced with beginning skill learners especially, but even with those elite athletes who have made modifications to an already well-learned motor program (e.g., changing a goalkeeper's approach for crossed balls).

*"The destiny of the game is shaped at practice."*
—Bill Beswick, Mental-Skills Trainer for English Premier Club County
(2001, p. 160)

## Quality Control

Quality control refers to the methods that coaches can utilize to determine the effectiveness of their coaching behaviors and practice sessions, and the ways in which they have attempted to assist their athletes in preparing and executing better in practice. Some methods are available that coaches can utilize to evaluate the effectiveness of the players in accomplishing the objectives of the training sessions. Charting, as described earlier in this chapter, may aid in motivation and accountability, and increase the quality of subsequent training sessions. Giving fitness tests before and during the season, formally and informally testing tactical and strategic awareness (plays, game strategy, assignments), and grading positional assignments in terms of execution and corrections will all help in evaluating practice quality.

Maintaining open lines of communication between players and coaches is another key determinant of optimal coach, player, and team effectiveness. Coaches who have players who feel comfortable talking with them about their feelings and perceptions (how things are going) will not only gain a better understanding of their athletes and team, but also a greater awareness of how their own attitudes and coaching behaviors are affecting their players. Coaches can set up formal and informal meetings with their players on a regular basis to evaluate not only players' progress, but also the coaching staff's progress regarding quality practice. It is worth repeating that coaches must connect and converse with players about subjects not limited to soccer. Today's players want their coaches to treat them as people, not just as players. Going the extra distance and developing relationships with players will go a long way to pushing the right buttons and helping players maximize their potential. Additionally, developing relationships and seeing players grow is one of the most rewarding aspects of coaching.

Coaches should also evaluate whether the amount of practice was beneficial in terms of positive training stress. If players begin to get overtrained (i.e., training stress exceeds the athletes' ability to recover adequately), not only will their performance suffer, but they also may experience emotional, psychological, and physiological consequences (Voight, 2003). See Chapter 8 for more information on the deleterious effects of excessive training stress and underrecovery on physical and mental well-being. Careful and smart implementation of overload and training stress should be evaluated by coaches after each training session. Schmidt and Wrisberg (2000) recommend using a checklist to evaluate the instructional strategies in terms of practice preparation (e.g., setting goals and identifying target skills), practice structure, presentation (e.g., clarifying expectations), and feedback.

Finally, coaches should also evaluate themselves and their staffs in terms of the amount of effort invested in the preparation and execution of practice sessions. As Anson Dorrance wrote, "...some coaches are no longer willing to make the emotional commitment needed to motivate players to attain the standard required of them to compete successfully at the highest level" (1996, p. 21). Due to this lack of emotional commitment, Dorrance reported that some coaches will not confront players who are not exerting maximal effort and thus end up having practice sessions that are easy and fun to run, but that do little to maximize learning and performance.

Courtesy of Tennessee Chattanooga Sports Information

Figure 15-6. Coaches who are proficient at coaching today's athletes establish respectful relationships and are better able to motivate and inspire their players.

# Chapter Summary

- A universal goal of coaches of all sports is to maximize the efficiency of practice time.
- Four major factors encapsulate the most important areas that both players and coaches should address in their effort to improve the quality of training: adopting a quality attitude, utilizing quality preparation techniques, practicing quality execution strategies, and taking the time after practice to complete a quality evaluation.
- The quality of individual and team practice performance relies on an interactive process between players and coaches. Both parties have certain responsibilities that they must meet for quality training to result.
- Some players view practice as an opportunity to play and improve, which denotes internally driven motivation, while others perceive practice as being externally driven and something that is "done to them."
- The quality of team and individual training can improve together, thus elevating the team and individual players' potential for quality play at game time.
- It is very important that coaches do all they can to create an atmosphere that fosters quality attitude, quality preparation, quality execution, and quality control.

# 16

# Quality Coaching:
# Beyond the X's and O's

Coaching "beyond the X's and O's" requires some additional time to adequately apply some of the important concepts and strategies contained within this book. Devoting time to strengthening players' mental toughness skills will be well worth it, because helping players automate their execution will greatly improve play, both on an individual and team level. The most important concepts and techniques for coaches to address with their players and team include an awareness of their technical and mental mechanics; the importance of automating their execution; the many performance barriers standing in the way of automatic execution; how these barriers specifically affect mechanical, mental, and performance proficiency via information processing and sequencing errors; and toughness-training exercises used to not only combat performance barriers, but also to overcome the debilitating effects of mechanical breakdowns. Adding these technical and mental mechanics to players' arsenals will better prepare them for game time, and also help them consistently execute on the practice field day in and day out.

This final chapter asks you to go a little further with your mental-game coaching by applying coaching-effectiveness practices. For youth coaches especially, this chapter details "developmental coaching" methods to assist young players with their physical, technical, mental, and social development. For competitive-level coaches, this chapter details the qualities and practices of effective sport leaders taken from research on coaching effectiveness and anecdotal reports from the coaches and athletes themselves.

# Youth Coaching Effectiveness

*"The mentality in youth sport needs to change. How can coaches teach valuable lessons about preparing youth for life when their value is based only on wins and losses?"*

—Steve Courson, Former NFL Player
(*Los Angeles Times,* April 28, 2005)

When coaches agree to coach youth players, a lot of responsibility is bestowed on these club or youth coaches. These coaches are responsible for the physical safety of their players, as well as for their social and psychological welfare via an educational and fun sport experience. Because some coaches are working with younger players, they are also responsible for helping them improve their basic movement patterns (see Chapter 1 for examples), as well as for teaching the fundamental technical skills of soccer. Coaches who only value the outcome will be doing their players a great disservice by not teaching them important fundamental movement and technical skills. A consequence of this type of coaching could include injury, because players may be pushed too hard physically in an attempt to play the game like their collegiate or professional idols before they have the requisite skill set. Psychologically, this type of coaching for youth players adversely affects their perceptions of competence, satisfaction, and motivation, and their willingness to continue playing the sport (even if the team wins).

Coaches should be aware of many age-specific, developmental concerns, especially if they coach players who are 16 years and younger. It has been reported in the developmental research that the quality and extent of a child's activity influence his motor and intellectual development. Although children's motor ability is partially determined by heredity, other factors combine to affect a child's potential, including activity level, environmental factors (e.g., nutrition, illness, rest), social factors (e.g., level of sport, support from family and coaches), psychological factors (e.g., stress, lack of self-confidence, coping ability, experience), and physical development (e.g., growth rates).

Although children proceed through predictable patterns of motor and intellectual development, they develop proficiency at different rates. Coaches and parents alike should be cautioned about "pushing" their young players to perform skills and activities before they are maturationally ready (physically, intellectually, and socially). Pushing a young athlete could result in accidents or physical injury, as well as in long-term effects, such as an attitude of fear, failure, low self-esteem, and low motivation to continue playing.

Based upon the human development, developmental psychology, motor development, motor learning, and pedagogy fields, the following considerations address specific developmental and age-related differences that coaches should be familiar with if working with youth. Figure 16-1 details the most important concerns and how coaches can best address these developmental needs, and thus become more responsible and more effective coaches and educators.

According to this research, younger athletes should not be rushed developmentally or technically. If players are not physically, mentally, or technically ready for such skills, forcing them to perform them will have a deleterious effect on the player in many areas. Players who are eight and younger also do not need to listen to a coach talk and talk. These young players are kinesthetically inclined and learn by doing, not by watching or listening. Coaches who get too caught up in hearing themselves talk will only lose their players and force them to entertain themselves, which usually equates to messing around with a teammate, which then upsets this coach due to them not being good listeners. It is not the players' fault in this case—let them play, coach!

What coaches say and how they treat individual players becomes critical for eight- and nine-year-old players. A coach who favors certain players, whether he realizes he is doing it or not, will be "caught" in the act by these perceptive youngsters. Coaches must be careful to play and treat everyone equally. At this age level, everyone should play the same amount of time and the atmosphere should be one of having fun and playing as a collective unit. Feedback and attention from coaches are cherished by players of this age, so coaches should not hold back in providing positive words, especially if they are deserved. This feedback becomes even more important, because players use this feedback to assist in developing their own sense of competence. The greater the feelings of competence with the game, the more motivated players become, leading them to continue to try new skills and play as hard as they can. The primary focus must be on developing a fun team climate, followed by the acquisition of fundamental physical and technical skills. Game outcome should not even be brought up in conversation. Thus, team most valuable player awards, tournament trophies, and other outcome-related awards should be kept in the stores until these players rise through the competitive levels.

Coaching 10 to 12 year olds can be the "best and worst of times." Coaches must realize that these players are changing developmentally, almost right in front of their eyes. Coaching the process of improving as a player should be paramount. Since most of these players' motor skills are well developed and automatic by this age, skill development should be a priority, especially in terms of proper execution and the functionality of movement and decision-making. Players at this age base a lot of their perceptions of competence on how they stack up against their peers, or in the case of sports, against their opponents. Coaches and parents should stress the importance of playing better than they did during the last practice or game, as opposed to being the

|  | **Developmental Concerns** | **Coach Applications** |
|---|---|---|
| **Middle Childhood (ages 6-12)** | | |
| 6-8 years old: | • importance of basic motor patterns (hand-eye coordination, footwork, balance, jumping)<br>• up to 8 years old, all learn kinesthetically rather than auditorily or visually | • important not to rush young athletes along—just getting the basic movement patterns is critical<br>• less *talking*, more *doing*—players learn by physical trial-and-error |
| 8-9 years old: | • prefer the use of *adult* feedback to judge their own competencies<br>• very much aware of individual differences (e.g., who's the best player and who's the worst)<br>• importance of modeling of same-sex parent<br>• very responsive to team/group activities | • need to hear confidence-enhancing feedback from coaches and parents<br>• aware of players who get treated differently<br>• look to parent(s) for modeling behaviors (comments made, overt behaviors before/during/after games) |
| 10-12 years old: | • begin perfectionistic thinking (get discouraged easily when not perfect—especially those with low confidence)<br>• will lose interest in activity if pressured<br>• prefer to be given more responsibility<br>• prefer to be talked to as an "equal"<br>• respond well to caring, mature adults<br>• rebellious and overcritical of self and others<br>• motor skills learned during early years are now automatic<br>• skill development now includes accuracy, coordination, and functionality of movements<br>• preference for *adult* feedback wanes—increase in reliance on peer comparison and evaluation | • coach and parents need to be careful not to associate athletic performance to their child's/player's personality (having a bad game does not equate to being a bad person—it is only a game)<br>• especially if a player has low self-confidence already, more pressure may drive him out of the game<br>• must be taught that making mistakes and failing (losing) are part of the process of learning your game and becoming a better athlete<br>• skill fundamentals are still critical—help make learning and practicing the FUNdamentals FUN<br>• stress the importance of performing better than *you* did yesterday—deemphasize social comparison |

Figure 16-1. Youth coaching effectiveness—developmental considerations

best player on the field. Coaches also must be careful to not associate performance on the field to player personality traits. For example, never tell a player that he is not mentally tough because he could not shake off a hard tackle. Also, players begin to adopt perfectionistic reasoning, so players must be taught that mistakes are only part of the process of becoming a better player, and this message needs to be repeated as often as possible with players at this age level.

| | **Developmental Concerns** | **Coach Applications** |
|---|---|---|
| **Adolescence (ages 12-17)** | | |
| 12-14 years old: | • period of *egocentrism*<br>• personal uniqueness, "untouchable"<br>• "imaginary audience"—believe they are center of attention, that people are either admiring or critical of them (In actuality, other adolescents are more concerned with being observed than with being the observer!)<br>• continued preference for peer comparison and evaluation<br>• emotional instability coupled with "know-it-all" mentality | • helpful for coaches to realize that teenagers do follow these particular "peculiarities," so they should not take it personally when players show these behaviors<br>• "calling players out" to make a point (singling them out for doing something wrong) usually does not have the desired effects, especially long term—players are more concerned with being embarrassed than they are about learning a lesson |
| 15-17 years old: | • begin to see themselves in "new light"; show empathy for others (volunteer activities), yet still display some egocentric thoughts and motives | • try to deemphasize comparing their performance with everyone else (uncontrollable and no-win game)—attempt to get players to use self-comparison (try to improve on what *you* did last time = internal criteria of success)<br>• provide feedback that is commensurate with degree of skill/drill difficulty (if easy skill, don't praise) |

Figure 16-1 (cont'd). Youth coaching effectiveness—developmental considerations

Once players hit adolescence, between the ages of 12 and 17, they vacillate between emotional instability and a "know-it-all" attitude. Although they will listen to the coach (for the most part), they prefer to receive feedback from their teammates and friends. Since adolescent players are so preoccupied with being "observed," penalizing players in front of their teammates is not an effective teaching tool. Players at this stage are engrossed in their own thinking and perceptions (egocentrism), so comparing them to other players or teams is not usually a viable form of motivation. It usually causes the players to become even more internal and self-conscious, and usually lowers player confidence, while increasing anxiety and tension (emotional instability). Toward the end of this stage, players show empathy toward others and begin to look beyond their own personal "worlds," yet they are still quite sensitive about public criticism, so coaches should continue to provide negative feedback on a personal basis.

# Competitive-Level Coaching Effectiveness

## Process Over Outcome

Many of today's schools, club organizations, and collegiate programs operate with a professional sport model, which features to a win-at-all-costs attitude. Steve Courson's quote cited earlier in this chapter mentions the importance of coaches changing their "mentality." Youth coaches becoming more aware of the developmental needs of their athletes, and specifically addressing these concerns in their coaching, is a step toward changing the current mentality. Another step that could be taken is for coaches to embrace the process rather than the outcome. At the collegiate level, the expectations are so very high that it is difficult for coaches and players not to feel pressure about winning another tournament or national championship. Yet, despite these high expectations, a program must grasp the importance of the *process* of becoming a national champion rather than focusing simply on the trophy. On a daily basis, the team should be reminded of what they need to do on the practice field to get one step closer to playing in the championship game.

These daily standards and goals are all part of the process of improving the team's ability to maximize their collective potential. Figure 16-2 illustrates the differences between an outcome focus and a process focus. Coaches who are always emphasizing the outcome are teaching their players that only a win can bring satisfaction and a sense of accomplishment. Teams that are coached with an outcome focus usually adopt the perceptions listed in Table 16-2. For example, when they play against a weaker team, players can let their guard down and not play to their utmost abilities, because they feel that it will not be necessary. When these teams play against tough teams, some players may perceive the game as a threat, since winning may not happen. With these teams, "moral" victories do not exist—even if they play very well, they cannot give themselves credit because the outcome was not accomplished (a loss). Also, if adversity strikes, such as a starter getting hurt or a new lineup being used, these players can get shaken because winning has been made even harder.

Conversely, process-orientated coaching can lead to more favorable perceptions by players. Remember, winning is somewhat of an uncontrollable. Players that embrace the importance of the process put the onus on themselves to play to their maximal

| Situational Perception | Outcome Focus | Process Focus |
|---|---|---|
| Playing a lesser opponent | Beat the team badly because we are the better team | Outplay the opponent; take care of our ball, ourselves and our game |
| Playing a tough, close match | View tough matches as a threat—we may lose | View this as a challenge; we want to test our skills |
| Playing a highly ranked team | Going to be tough to beat this team | It's all about our team—let's play our game |
| Playing a lesser opponent | Chances that our team will play down to their level due to overconfidence | Focus on playing our game and improve upon our weaknesses |
| Playing with a key starter injured | How can we compete? How can we win? | Now we really have to play together; what more can we each contribute? |
| Starting slow versus a lesser opponent | We can pick it up at any time | We have to get back to the game plan |
| Starting slow versus a tough opponent | What's going on? Finger-pointing, blaming, even panic | We have come back before; go back to the game plan |
| Playing with a new lineup | We need time to get used to each other: could be tough to get a win | Let's help each other play our team game |
| Playing a tough schedule | Going to be tough to go undefeated; who can we beat? | Each game will challenge us to play to our utmost; we must be ready to play |

Figure 16-2. What game do you play? Process versus outcome

capacities. Whether playing against lesser or better teams, process-orientated players take care of their own side of the field first, and then let the outcome take care of itself. The focus is on improving the team's product (team performance), so if adversity strikes, the team is ready to continue their pursuit of playing well, one pass at a time. Such teams do not feel threatened by higher-ranked programs, and in fact look forward to the challenge of testing their play against the best. Helping players adopt this type of team philosophy takes time, continual follow-up, and productive feedback. Most players are coached under the win-at-all-costs professional sport model in their school and club teams, so they may be somewhat resistant to changing their mindset. But once players allow the "process" to guide them, they will begin giving themselves credit for good performances (regardless of outcome), and attempt to play better each practice and improve from one game to the next.

## Rules Without Relationships

Coaching today's athlete is much different than it was 20 years ago, or even 10 years ago. Anecdotal evidence includes feedback from coaches who consistently state that the one major difference between athletes from the past and today's athletes is the importance placed on the coach-athlete relationship (Voight, 2000c). "Rules without relationships lead to rebellion" is a popular title for presentations on the topic. Team rules and standards will not be accepted nor adhered to if a real player-coach relationship is not developed. The relationship developed between the coach and his players must be based upon things beyond just athletic performance. This change does not dictate that the coach must become a best friend to his players, but their bond must exist beyond the soccer field if players are to give their all to the team and the coach. Pete Carroll, head football coach at USC, stated that "the relationship is the best way to get the result. I'm convinced that developing and maintaining healthy relationships is the best way, if not the only way, to get where you want to go in life." Coaches at all levels of sport must put in the necessary time and effort to get to know their players as people and players. Coaches who invest in their players will see them invest in the team pursuit and their coaches. Do not become one of the many coaches who learned this lesson the hard way—by having players quit on them, player revolts, team dissension, player dissatisfaction, and teams underperforming.

## Teachable Moments: Productive Coaching

This term, "teachable moment," is explained in Chapter 15, but it is important enough to repeat and expand upon in the youth sport setting. Finding moments when players do things right is a valuable teaching strategy, and is referred to as productive coaching. When it is deserved, productive feedback can help positively influence a player's competence, self-confidence, and intrinsic motivation. Competence has been defined as a player's skill capabilities, as well as his knowledge of the intricacies of his sport. A player's self-confidence consists of his belief in his abilities. Most coaches believe that confidence is at the core of playing to potential. A player's intrinsic motivation refers to his drive for continued efforts at improvement and achievement. Coaches can have a profound influence on young competitors, through productive coaching methods, specifically their instructional behaviors, use of keen observation, careful use of feedback, reinforcement, and motivation, and the development of a process-oriented team climate.

### Instructional Behaviors

An often-used coaching phrase states that "the game is the best teacher." Coaches should let players play rather than listen to how it should be done. Some coaches simply talk too much. To aid in educating players on the process, coaches can TARGET their practices:

T = Task: Use a variety of activities and exercises that are challenging, yet appropriate for the developmental and ability levels of the players.

A = Authority: Involve players in decision making, such as choosing some activities for practice or helping select uniforms. Athletes at age 16 and older prefer that coaches train them in competitive drills and practices. They may want some say, but players at this age want the coach to dictate the standard and hold them to it.

R = Recognition: Coaches should reward individual improvement and effort, while simultaneously focusing on the athlete's self-worth and confidence.

G = Grouping: Technical practice should move from individual, to small group, to large group work. The smaller the group, the more reps with the ball each player gets.

E = Evaluation: Individual standards of performance should measure progress, not simply outcome-based results such as winning or losing. Even in a loss, coaches should evaluate the good aspects of play.

T = Timing: Coaches should provide time for learning and improvement by utilizing teaching progressions that move from simple to complex, and by providing "lots and lots" of reps. Time should be spent practicing, not standing in line waiting for a turn. Repetitions and overlearning are critical for younger players.

Figure 16-3. Competitive youth coaches can improve player execution by being on TARGET.

Coaches should not only look for "teachable moments" and error-correction opportunities, but also observe and listen for particular verbal and nonverbal statements and behaviors among the players. They could be conveying important information—namely levels of competence, self-confidence, and persistence.

Coaches must be cognizant of player statements such as "I can't do this," "I don't know what to do most of the time," or "I am so stupid." Players may be making these statements out of their frustration about not being competent enough to play on this team. Players must be told that learning their skills will take a lot of time and practice. Players must not be admonished for making mistakes at this level of play. Players should be able to use trial and continuous error correction without penalty (laps, getting yelled at). Getting on players will only have an adverse effect on their confidence and competence, and possibly drive them away from a game they once loved. In a similar vain, talk like "I stink," or "I am the worst player on this field" could denote players who are really struggling with their confidence. Upon hearing these statements, coaches should attempt to get players to think about improving upon their last performance rather than comparing themselves with others, since they have no control over how their teammates or opponents play.

In terms of going too far with boosting player confidence, coaches should be cautioned about only praising worthy performances. You must be careful not to praise easy tasks that the player does in him sleep or it will leave him with the perception that you think he is not very skillful (i.e., accomplishing an easy task is challenging for him). Players at all competition and age levels are very perceptive and are always looking for real or mixed messages from adults and coaches. A player's sense of competence and confidence is greatly enhanced when they accomplish challenging tasks. Coaches should continue to set high, yet realistic standards that their players could accomplish if they put forth their best effort.

Another issue for coaches to be aware of is when they notice that a player's effort is dropping off, which could be due to something going on at home or school. This player is probably having trouble "letting go" or "moving on" from the issue. Having a rapport with your players will help them to open up when they do have problems. A decrease in work rate could also signal some dissatisfaction with you, your coaching, or their teammates. The sooner these issues can be discussed the better. The player could easily be getting some "bad" information or "misperceptions" from their parents, so both parties should be addressed so that no miscommunication takes place. Players may begin to miss practices and games (with faulty excuses) as a way of avoiding a threatening situation, such as a problem with a teammate or coach, or a fear of making mistakes or letting their parents down. Getting them to talk about how things are going is very important. Players who avoid playing could also be close to being on their way out. They may not be getting what they most prefer out of the experience, such as a relationship with his coach and teammates, improved play, or challenging play. Find out *why* your players play, so you can be in a better position to help them meet their expectations and preferences.

*Feedback and Reinforcement*

To improve upon the use of contingent praise, it is important to offer the type of praise that gives players a standard to achieve, while also providing skill-relevant feedback. General feedback, like "nice job," is not even close to providing important information. Feedback such as, "You passed the ball right where it needed to be for that particular play. Let's try that again," is much better and much more informative. The following list includes tips that coaches can use to improve upon the use of productive feedback:

- Use "I" messages instead of "you" messages. This technique helps to reduce a defensive stance from the player. For example, "I see you not getting into a supportive defensive position quickly enough."
- Always avoid using sarcasm in a learning environment.
- Reward what you want, not what you do not want. Sometimes, ignoring a negative will take care of the problem, especially if the player is not getting the attention he is looking for. If you can't ignore it, try to step in without making a big deal and devote as little time as possible to the situation. Attention is what athletes want most of the time, so if they see you giving your attention and positive feedback to players who are doing the right things, and not to players doing the wrong things, they may actually get the message.
- Be mindful of how you offer coaching points, such as by pointing your finger at a player with a demanding tone or using a facial expression or body language that emits a negative connotation. The message may be great, but the player may not be listening because he is too distracted by the nonverbals ("Why is he so mad at me?"). What coaches do and how they do it speaks volumes, more so than what they actually say.

The best way to motivate players is to keep them working to improve their game every day, as well as by doing the following:

- Get to know your players and give them some time outside of soccer (ask them about school, family, interests, etc.).
- Plan ways to improve team cohesion and increase motivation (it will not just happen).
- Have training sessions that are organized, competitive, and full of reps.
- Establish a standard of practice behaviors and hold players accountable to it. Players need to be held accountable for their roles and responsibilities, day in and day out. Once every player feels like a contributing member of the team, good things will happen.

- If the situation dictates, showing players your frustration and disappointment can be beneficial (it will show them you care), but coaches should never attack player's personality or character.

The following list details how coaches should not attempt to motivate their players. By using these methods, coaches may see an immediate behavior change based upon fear and resentment from the players, but these techniques will wreak havoc on the coach's character, credibility, and future leadership ability. Chapter 12 addresses some of these points in the "10 commandments of team communication."

- Intimidation ("If you don't go out and play hard I will cut you.")
- Threats ("If you make the same mistake again you won't play for a long time.")
- Criticism and sarcasm ("That's the worst soccer I have ever seen." "My five year old knows soccer better than all of you combined.")
- Guilt ("All the time I've put into training you and this is what I get in return?")
- Physical abuse ("We'll run the entire next practice if...")
- Fear ("I want them to fear me because they work harder.")
- Arrogance ("I am the coach. What can one of my players tell me that I don't already know?")
- Negativity ("I'm doing my players a big favor by treating them like this. It is preparing them for the real world.")
- Favoritism ("Every good coach treats his better players differently from the rest."). It is important for coaches to tell their players that everyone will be treated fairly. It is very difficult to treat each player equally, so coaches should focus on developing a relationship and rapport with each team member and try to be as fair as possible with them.

*Team Climate*

It is important for coaches to develop their own coaching philosophy and vision for the team, which together should act as a compass as they embark on the journey of leading their team. Ask yourself questions such as, "What is my coaching philosophy? What is the main *goal* of my coaching? What is the goal for the season?" Hopefully, player development, fun, and skill improvement make up the top three coaching goals and priorities, especially for youth coaches. These goals should not only be passed onto the players and their parents, but they should also be practiced and enforced during every practice and game. Making sure that every player plays, is involved with each drill, is given opportunities for practice reps, and is given appropriate reinforcement (in proportion to the difficulty of the skill or activity) are ways of putting these standards to work. Other elements of an effective team climate include error correction (how coaches help players learn from mistakes) and postgame and postpractice evaluations.

How a team treats each other, especially the reserve players, can make a great difference in its effectiveness. Mick Haley, who has won volleyball national titles at Texas and USC, stresses the importance of challenging every player, especially the reserves. Anson Dorrance, a highly successful women's soccer coach at UNC, also highlights the need for teams to respect their reserves, as they are the foundation of any competitive program. Coach Dorrance has stated that the treatment of reserve players is one of the key components of team chemistry and effective leadership. The important questions to ask of yourself and your team include the following. The answers to these questions could be at the heart of your successes or failures.

- What are the attitudes of the reserve players?
- Are reserve players respected for their contributions?
- How do the starting players view and treat reserve players?
- How do you (as the coach) treat your reserve players compared to how you treat your starters?

## Postgame Evaluations

A valuable teachable moment, which often goes by without notice or is not used effectively enough, is the postgame/postpractice evaluation. Both players and coaches can utilize this time to do the following:
- Take note of what they are feeling and thinking about the performance
- Realize what got them to the outcome (good, neutral, or poor)
- Think about how was their play compared with play in the past (improvement, neutral, or "back a few steps")
- List what aspects of the "team" game were good, neutral, or poor
- List specific aspects that will need to be targeted in training

How these points are addressed, attributed, and emphasized to players can have a profound effect (good or bad) on an athlete's interpretation of the outcome, which then strongly influences his mindset, attitude, and motivation for future performance (practice and game play). For example, a loss can still be a desirable outcome if the team gave all it had and improved in certain areas of emphasis; the opposite applies to a "sloppy" win, when the team simply went through the motions and did not work hard or improve their team game, yet still got the win. Coaches set this tone with their postgame feedback. Sport psychologist Mark Anshel (1990) wrote that, "Coaches are responsible for making an honest and accurate evaluation of good and poor performance so that the causes of the end result can be objectively determined." Some common examples of how coaches assess the causes of the outcome (win, loss) could include the following (Anshel, 1990):

- Ability attributes
  - ✓ "We played well today."
  - ✓ "We've been keeping possession great recently."
  - ✓ "We did not play well at this tournament."
  - ✓ "We are mentally tougher than most teams."

- Task difficulty attributes
  - ✓ "We really battled against their bigger defenders today, but they won most of the challenges."
  - ✓ "Their attack was just the best I have seen in a long time."
  - ✓ "We played well despite facing players two years older."
  - ✓ "We just beat one of the best teams at this tournament."

- Effort attributes
  - ✓ "We were outworked this game."
  - ✓ "When we attack the flanks we are tough to beat."
  - ✓ "We have to be aggressive to win this championship."
  - ✓ "We didn't put the effort in during practice this week to adequately prepare."

- Luck attributes
  - ✓ "Luck was not on our side today."
  - ✓ "The officials were making all the wrong calls today."
  - ✓ "That team pulled off some 'career' possessions and goals today."
  - ✓ "We just didn't have it today."

The research that has been conducted on success and failure attributions has revealed much about how students and athletes perceive what they are being told and how these perceptions relate to their future actions. For example, younger athletes who attribute losses/failure/undesirable outcomes to *low ability* tend to have higher levels of anxiety, lower levels of confidence, and are more at risk to drop out of sport. Also, athletes who continually attribute, or are told by their coaches, that losses are due to their lack of *ability*, tend to lose motivation and drive to continue striving to practice and perform. It is wiser to attribute undesirable outcomes (losses, poor performances with a win) to *low effort*, since players can always change this attribute, or to *luck* and the opponents' *ability*.

Helping players realize that unsuccessful performances should also be attributed to inadequate training, a lack of continual effort throughout the match, inappropriate strategy, or an inadequate focus in critical times is crucial, since these *internal* attributes can all be changed. Coaches who continually attribute losses to low ability will demotivate their players and create more inconsistent, poor play. Most athletes perform better in future contests when they attribute the outcome to effort rather than ability. Attributing failure to ability again leads to lower confidence and a decreased motivation to continue putting in effort. Effort should always be mentioned as the most important factor in skill improvement. If skill is emphasized too much, those athletes who are not as skilled as the others will assume that they "don't have it" and never will.

Coaches must be careful about getting too involved in blaming others for losses and failures, such as officiating or a superior opponent. Although it was stated earlier that attributing losses to outside factors can protect younger players' sense of competence and confidence, if outside factors are always mentioned as a cause of a loss it can demotivate athletes in the long run. Players may feel good at the time to get past the loss, but if they keep hearing about this "impossible opponent" they will begin to question their ability. Again, external factors like luck and a tough opponent can be used sparingly to save a team's ego and confidence as needed, such as after a great effort when the team battled tremendous adversity to keep the game close. If coaches elect to use external factors like luck and task difficulty, they should try to state it in positive terms, such as, "We played okay today, but the opponents just pulled out some lucky shots" (luck) or "Hold your heads high. You were beaten by a very good team today" (task difficulty).

As mentioned in Figure 16-1, coaches should be aware of the developmental considerations of their players, especially when comparing one player to another (social comparison). Only a few athletes actually can handle being compared to other players ("Why can't you dribble like Torie?"). Most athletes will question their own ability instead of getting motivated to work harder to play like Torie. It should not be a problem to tell an athlete that she is not starting and Torie is starting due to some objective performance criteria, because this statement helps the athlete understand the specific areas in which she is deficient. It is the subjective statements that hurt players personally, which then adversely affect their confidence and motivation to continue to play.

Finally, coaches must be honest and real with their time-out/game-break/postgame comments. If players failed to execute the skills, let them know rather than blaming luck or citing a good opponent all the time. The important point is that coaches need to think about what to say and what message they want to get across. When coaches let their emotions run the show, and say what will make them feel better (cathartic coaching), they may lose several players when all is said and done. Remember, coaching today's athlete is very different from the Bob Knight days of yelling, pushing, and cajoling. Players want to be treated with respect and be given responsibility. Especially during time-outs and postgame evaluations, coaches' attributions should be phrased in terms that educate—"We need to do a better job of getting to every second ball."—rather than in terms that attack and destroy, such as "This is the worst soccer that has ever been played."

# Final Thoughts

A sport like soccer demands a lot from its participants, especially with the speed of play and the hard tackling/defending at the higher levels of the game. This game can be a tremendous test for players because of the momentum swings and the importance of every tackle, pass, and shot. Players and teams that are able to let go of the previous play and focus on the next possession will have an advantage over most of their opponents. Players and teams that are able to put in quality, consistent training sessions will be at an even greater advantage. This book is the first to specifically address these important issues while providing hands-on, tried-and-true strategies specific to soccer to assist your players and teams in maximizing their capacities and potential.

By helping your players become mentally tougher, you will enable them to become comfortable being uncomfortable, remain confident, composed, and resilient, and be able to train with consistent focus and effort. For some players, these skills are automatic. But for the majority of players, these skills must be practiced, much like passing, heading, and shooting. Once players are able to incorporate these mental skills on a daily basis without hesitation, they are well on their way to performing to their potential. These players will be able to achieve great things, like playing to the best of their ability, playing on teams that play for each other, winning a championship, and maybe even making a visit to the White House.

# References and Recommended Reading

Anderson, R.J. (2003). Sweat & smiles. *Coaching Management,* 11(9), 18–22.

Anshel, M.H. (1990). *Sport Psychology: From Theory to Practice.* Scottsdale, AZ: Gorsuch Scarisbrick, Publishers.

Baechle, T.R. & Earle, R.W. (Eds.) (2000). *Essentials of Strength Training and Conditioning.* Colorado Springs, CO: NSCA.

Baechle, T.R., Earle, R.W., & Wathen, J. (2000). Resistance training. In T.R. Baechle & R.W. Earle (Eds.) *Essentials of Strength Training and Conditioning* (pp. 395–426). Colorado Springs, CO: NSCA.

Beswick, B. (2001). *Focused for Soccer.* Champaign, IL: Human Kinetics.

Bompa, T. (1983). *Periodization of Training.* Champaign, IL: Human Kinetics .

Bowden, B., Bowden, T., & Brown, B. (1996). *Winning's Only Part of the Game.* New York, NY: Warner Books.

Carron, A.V., Spink, K.S., & Prapavessis, H. (1997). Team building and cohesiveness in the sport and exercise setting: Use of indirect interventions. *Journal of Applied Sport Psychology,* 9, 61–72.

Chichester, B. (2002, Spring). The dangers of dehydration. *Hydrate,* 11.

Didenger, R. (1995). *Game Plans for Success.* Chicago, IL: Contemporary Books.

Dorfman, H. (2003). *Coaching the Mental Game.* Lanham, MD: Taylor Trade Publishing.

Dorrance, A. (1996). *Training Soccer Champions.* Raleigh, NC: JTC Sports.

Dufresne, C. (2004, May). Revolution stops here. *Los Angeles Times,* D12.

Emma, T. (2003). *Peak Performance Training for Sports.* Monterey, CA: Coaches Choice Publishers.

Fishman, M.G. & Oxendine, J.B. (1998). Motor skill learning for effective coaching and performance. In J. Williams (Ed.) *Applied Sport Psychology: Personal Growth to Peak Performance* (3rd ed.; pp. 13–27). New York: Macmillan.

Fitzgerald, M. (2003, August). The top 10 sports science tips. *Triathlete,* 56–59.

Hardy, C.J. & Crace, R.K. (1997). Foundations of team building: Introduction to team building primer. *Journal of Applied Sport Psychology, 9*, 1–10.

Henschen, K.P. (1986). Athletic staleness and burnout: Diagnosis, prevention, and treatment. In J.M. Williams (Ed.) *Applied Sport Psychology* (pp. 327–342). Palo Alto, CA: Mayfield.

*Hydrate* (2002, Spring). Power up with H2O, 18.

Janssen, J. (2002). *Championship Team Building.* Cary, NC: Winning the Mental Game.

Janssen, J., and Dale, G. (2001). *The 7 Secrets of Successful Coaches.* Cary, NC: Winning the Mental Game.

Jenkins, R. (2003). *Mental Preparation for Quarterbacks.* www.TopGunQBAcademy.com

Jordan, M. (1994). *I Can't Accept not Trying.* New York, NY: Harper Collins.

Kirkendall, D. (1996). Physical and tactical demands of soccer. In T. Schum (Ed.) *Coaching Soccer* (pp. 251–253). Indianapolis, IN: Masters Press.

Kluka, D. (2004). *Talent Identification.* Presentation book at AVCA national convention. Long Beach, CA.

Lencione, P. (2002). *The 5 Dysfunctions of a Team.* New York, NY: Macmillan.

Liddane, L. (2002, February 4). Feed your muscles. *Daily News,* 42.

Loehr, J. (1994). *The New Toughness Training Manual for Sports.* New York, NY: Plume-Penguin.

Loehr, J. et al. (October, 2001). "Expanding Player Capacities." Workshop presented at the Association for the Advancement of Applied Sport Psychology, Orlando, FL.

*Los Angeles Times* (2003a). October 31. D2.

*Los Angeles Times* (2003b). September 24. D12.

*Los Angeles Times* (2003c). August 30. D10.

*Los Angeles Times* (2004). November 27. D2.

*Los Angeles Times* (2005). April 28. D1.

McCallum, J. (2001). The gang's all here. *Sports Illustrated,* 75–81.

McCann, S. (2002). A model of offensive and defensive mental skills. *United States Olympic Coach.*

McKown, M. & Malone, K. (2003). *Strength Training with Dumbbells.* Germany: Myers and Myers.

Miller, S. (2003). *Hockey Tough*. Champaign, IL: Human Kinetics.

Moore, B. (1998). Confidence. In M.A. Thompson, R.A. Vernacchia, & W.E. Moore (Eds.) *Case Studies in Sport Psychology* (pp. 63–88). Dubuque, IA: Kendall/Hunt Publishing.

Murphy, M. (1996). *The Achievement Zone: 8 Skills for Winning all the Time from the Playing Field to the Boardroom*. New York, NY: G.P. Putnam's Sons.

Nideffer, R. (1989). *Attentional Control Training for Sport*. Los Gatos, CA: Performance Services.

Nideffer, R. (1976). Test of attentional and interpersonal style. *Journal of Personality and Social Psychology, 34*, 394–404.

Potach, D.H. & Chu, D.A. (2000). Plyometric training. In T.R. Baechle & R.W. Earle (Eds.) *Essentials of Strength Training and Conditioning* (pp. 427–470). Colorado Springs, CO: NSCA.

Orlick, T. (2000). *In Pursuit of Excellence* (3rd ed.). Champaign, IL: Human Kinetics.

Osbourne, T. & Ravizza, K. (1988). Nebraska's 3 R;s: 1 play at a time pre- performance routine for collegiate football. *The Sport Psychologist, 5*, 256–265.

Reimers, K. & Ruud, J. (2000). Nutritional factors in health and performance. In T.R. Baechle & R.W. Earle, R.W. (Eds.) *Essentials of Strength Training and Conditioning*. Colorado Springs, CO: NSCA.

Riley, P. (1993). *The Winner Within*. New York, NY: Putnam.

Roberts, P. (2001, May). Ed Burke's got a rocket in his pita pocket. *Outside, 87*.

Schmidt, A., Peper, E., & Wilson, V. (2001). Strategies for training concentration. In J. Williams (Ed.) *Applied Sport Psychology* (4th ed.; pp. 333–346). Mountain View, CA: Mayfield.

Schmidt, R.A., & Wrisberg, C.A. (2000). *Motor Learning and Performance* (2nd ed.). Champaign, IL: Human Kinetics.

Silva, J. (1990). An analysis of the training stress syndrome in competitive athletics. *Journal of Applied Sport Psychology, 2*, 5–20.

Smith, D. (1999, September). Overtraining in sport. Symposium presented at the annual meeting of the Association for the Advancement of Applied Sport Psychology Annual Conference. Banff, Canada.

Stellino, V. (2002, October). Jags try positive approach. *Florida Times Union*, D10.

*USA Today* (2003, October 17). Viking players have become true believers in what their coach says, 2C.

*USC Hospitality Services Pamphlet* (2003).

Vealey, R. (2002). Sport confidence from a social-cognitive perspective: Extending and blending research and practice. Presented at October AAASP Conference. Tucson, AZ.

Voight, M.R. (2004). Offensive and defensive mental skill survey. *Coaching Volleyball, 2,* 15–18.

Voight, M.R. (2003). Combating training stress syndromes to improve the quality of strength and conditioning training and performance. *Strength and Conditioning Journal,* 22–29.

Voight, M.R. (2002). Improving the quality of practice: Coach and player responsibilities. *Journal of Physical Education, Recreation, & Dance, 73,* 43–48.

Voight, M.R. (2001). A team building intervention program study with university teams. *Journal of Sport Behavior, 24,* 420–431.

Voight, M.R. (2000c). *A structural model of the determinants, personal and situational influences, and the consequences of athlete dissatisfaction.* Unpublished dissertation. University of Southern California.

Voight, M.R. (2000b). Postseason play: Mentally preparing for the distractions. *Coaching Women's Basketball,* 10–12.

Voight, M.R. (2000a). When the work doesn't get done: Important consequences for players and coaches. *Coaching Women's Basketball,* 12–13.

Waite, P. (2002). Giving players and teams the competitive edge. In D. Shondell & C. Reynaud (Eds.) *The Volleyball Coaching Bible* (pp. 300–325). Champaign, IL: Human Kinetics.

Walsh, B., & Dickey, G. (1990). *Building a Champion.* New York, NY: St. Martin's Paperbacks.

Williams, P. (1997). *The Magic of Teamwork.* Nashville, TN: Thomas Nelson Publishers.

Woods, T. (2001). *How I Play Golf.* New York, NY: Macmillan Publishers.

Yukelson, D. (1997). Principles of effective team building interventions in sport: A direct services approach at Penn State University. *Journal of Applied Sport Psychology, 9,* 73–96.

Ziegler, S. (2002). Attentional training: Our best kept secret. *Journal of Physical Education, Recreation, and Dance, 73,* 26–30.

## Additional Resources

Association for the Advancement of Applied Sport Psychology
www.aaasponline.org

National Strength and Conditioning Association
www.nsca-lift.org

Nutrition Counseling Education Services
www.ncescatalog.com

For more information regarding mental-toughness training and workshops, contact:

Dr. Voight's Sport Psychology Consulting and Workshops:

email: coach@drmikevoight.com

Web: www.drmikevoight.com

# About the Author

**Mike Voight,** Ph.D., CSCS, is a premier sport psychology-performance consultant with extensive experience working with athletes and teams from all types and levels of competitive sport. Mike has had the privilege of working with many collegiate, elite, Olympic, and professional athletes. Some notables include college and professional national champions, junior/national team soccer and volleyball players, Olympic athletes from diving, volleyball, and figure skating, and professional athletes from volleyball, hockey, basketball, soccer, and golf, as well as a Heisman trophy winner.

Mike is an assistant professor in the Physical Education-Human Performance Department at Central Connecticut State University. Previously, he was a lecturer in the Physical Education Department at the University of Southern California. He was also the sport psychology-performance consultant for USC for nine years, having worked with athletes and coaches from soccer, volleyball, football, basketball, rowing, golf, tennis, swimming, water polo, and diving teams. Despite his new academic position, Mike will continue to consult with several teams from USC. Being a certified sport psychology consultant (AAASP), a certified strength and conditioning specialist (CSCS), and a former Division I collegiate coach, Mike integrates the most recent research and applications from the sport sciences to provide the most comprehensive, cutting-edge performance-enhancement programming.

Along with his private consulting practice at Rivers Landing (LA Fitness, Trillium Sports Medicine) in Springfield (MA), Mike has been a speaker and consultant to top Division I universities throughout the nation, including University of Texas, Vanderbilt, Harvard, UCONN, CCSU, Virginia, Oregon State, UNC-Charlotte, CAL, Rutgers, UMASS, and UT Chattanooga. Dr. Voight has been fortunate to consult with some of the best coaching staffs from the collegiate and professional ranks, most notably the coaching staffs from the New York Liberty and Washington Mystics (WNBA) and the Los Angeles Kings (NHL).

Dr. Voight also spends considerable time conducting sport performance–related research and presenting his applied work at national and international conferences. His published articles can be found in sport psychology, sport science, and coaching journals. He is an editorial board member for the *International Journal for Sport Science and Coaching,* and a reviewer for an applied research journal. Additionally, he is the series editor for a complete line of mental toughness training books through Coaches Choice. An educator, researcher, presenter, writer, and applied practitioner, he is listed in the United States Olympic Committee's Sport Psychology Registry.

Mike resides in East Longmeadow, MA, with his wife, Jenny, their son, Bradley Cole, and their twins, Allyson and Julieann.